Keeping It All Together

The Preservation and Care of Historic Furniture

by Marc A. Williams

First Edition, 1988.

The following illustrations are copyrighted 1987 by Marc A. Williams:

Chapter 6, Figures 4, 6B, 12, 14, 15, 16; Chapter 7, Figures 9A and B, 10, 11, 14, 15A and B, 16; Chapter 8, Figures 1, 2, 3, 4, 6, 10, 13, 14, 15, 16, 17A and B, 19, 20; Chapter 9, Figure 2

Library of Congress Catalog Card Number 88-60428

ISBN 0-9603290-1-3

Published by Ohio Antique Review, Inc.
                12 East Stafford Avenue
                Worthington, Ohio 43085

About The Author

Marc A. Williams is the Chief Furniture Conservator at the Conservation Analytical Laboratory of the Smithsonian Institution, Washington, D.C. After completing undergraduate studies in American decorative arts and chemistry, he received his Master's Degree from the Winterthur Museum/University of Delaware Art Conservation Program. Following an internship in the Furniture Conservation Department of the Museum of Fine Arts, Boston, Mr. Williams served as Director of Furniture Conservation Services in Haverhill, Massachusetts. Currently, in addition to his duties as head of CAL/SI's Furniture Conservation department, he administers its Furniture Conservation Training Program.

Contents

Acknowledgements

A number of individuals assisted with the preparation of this booklet and I would like to thank those whose involvement was greatest. First and foremost is Jolene Cody, former Assistant Editor of *Antique Review*. Jolene's inspiration helped create the concept of the series of articles that led to this booklet and her assistance with the final editing of many of the articles was appreciated greatly. Don Williams, Furniture Conservator at the Conservation Analytical Laboratory, Smithsonian Institution, deserves special thanks for his help in technical review. Eleanor McMillan, Supervisory Conservator, CAL, SI, tirelessly offered many helpful editorial suggestions. Doc Dougherty, Photographer, SI, deserves credit for his heroic printing efforts, often under rushed deadlines. Lambertus van Zelst, Director of CAL, must be thanked for his continued support of conservation consciousness-raising activities, such as this booklet. Finally, I would like to thank Charles Muller, Editor of *Antique Review,* for his helpfulness in transforming the articles into this booklet.

Foreword

This booklet is intended to assist the owners of historic furniture and wooden objects, be they homeowners, collectors, dealers or curators, in the massive responsibility of caring for their pieces. In the past, this subject has been approached in a haphazard manner, with many of the published and verbal suggestions being based on heresay and myth. As a result, the custodian of historic objects is faced with a complicated and often conflicting array of information which is as likely as not to raise more questions than it answers.

The structure of this booklet is such that each chapter builds upon preceding ones. Information is presented that allows the reader to understand why deterioration occurs and, with this knowledge, to further the cause of preservation. For this reason, it is advisable to read the booklet in sequential order.

The contents of the booklet were originally a series of articles that appeared in *Antique Review* between August 1986 and August 1987. They have been edited slightly to facilitate publication in a single volume.

Chapter 1

Furniture Conservation: an Introduction and History

Everything deteriorates, including historic objects, and nothing can be done to stop this eventuality. Must an owner, however, be resigned to a lifetime of restoration and repair? While it is true that deterioration of artistic and historic objects cannot be stopped, it can be slowed significantly. This booklet will provide a basis of understanding upon which the owner can draw to reduce the need for restoration. It is the goal of the art conservation profession to do just that.

Conservation

What is conservation? Stated simply, it is the *preservation* (minimization of future deterioration), *stabilization* (consolidation of existing deterioration), and *restoration* (repair of existing deterioration) of historic and artistic objects. The causes of deterioration are studied to better understand how they can be minimized. Environmental conditions are monitored and adjusted to approach the optimum level. Treatment materials and processes are tested for stability, safety with regard to the objects for which they are intended, and effectiveness. Education and dissemination of information are promoted, as is fastidious documentation of treatments. To gain a better understanding of the conservation profession, it would be helpful to look at its history. A general overview will be given, followed by specific examination of the field of furniture conservation.

History

Ever since the existence of the first material objects thousands of years ago, individuals have been involved with their repair. Early objects were made, and repaired, by their owners. Soon after economic specialization allowed the existence of artisans, individuals skilled in repair evolved. Most were part-time repairpersons and themselves producing artisans, as exemplified by the advertisements of 18th century Philadelphia cabinetmakers which listed furniture repair as one of the services offered. Undoubtedly, repair procedures at this time were intended to make the object again functional and aesthetically whole, as it originally had been.

In the mid-19th century, a transformation occurred in the way society viewed its objects. The earlier societal value that resulted in objects being utilitarian and aesthetically representative of current style was transformed to embrace an additional value in which objects were desired to be historically chic. No longer were objects simply repaired so as to be "good as new." Old was now "in" and there was a desire for history and an appearance of age. This subtle shift in attitude marks the roots of the conservation profession.

Early "restorers," as they were called, used methods and techniques that were handed down from one generation to the next and were undoubtedly borrowed from the appropriate craft traditions. Due to the effect of the guild system in Europe, many of these techniques and materials were kept secret and a mystique grew about restoration. At about the same time, economic factors came into play. Values of historic pieces were rising and demand was high. Restoration ethics (or lack thereof) encouraged the execution of invisible repairs and visual "improvements" to pieces, culminating in an entire industry which produced fakes and pieces assembled from old parts.

By the late 19th and early 20th centuries, artistic and historic objects were being examined in an academic and scholarly manner. Their importance as cultural documents was being realized and, as such, the need to preserve them in an unaltered state became evident. A number of individuals in the museum world recognized the benefit of looking at deterioration and preservation from an interdisciplinary perspective. They noted that science, particularly chemistry, could be applied to better understand the compositional nature of a piece. This knowledge, combined with anthropological and art historical study of the object and its original production techniques led to a better understanding of deterioration processes. While the secrecy of traditional restoration had prohibited information exchange, early conservators became committed to open communication of ideas and techniques. For the first time, preservation and treatment processes could be examined objectively.

As the conservation profession developed, it borrowed techniques of examination and analysis from many different fields. These included the use of X-radiographs to view hidden areas of a piece, and the determination of an unidentified finish by infra-red spectrometry. Much original conservation research was now begun. All of this led to the realization that many traditional restoration techniques, while providing immediate visual or structural improvement, were actually causing long-term deterioration. Research and testing advanced at an ever-increasing pace.

In an attempt to facilitate communication among conservators, the International Institute for Conservation of Historic and Artistic Works (IIC, 6 Buckingham St., London WC2N 6BA, England) was formed in 1950. The American Group of IIC formed shortly thereafter, becoming the American Institute for Conservation of Historic and Artistic Works (AIC, 3545 Williamsburg Lane, NW, Washington, DC 20008) in 1973.

Training

Early training opportunities for conservators consisted primarily of hands-on experience similar to a traditional crafts apprenticeship. In the 1920s and 1930s, the Fogg Art Museum at Harvard began offering a few courses in art techniques and conservation to supplement the hands-on experience that could be gained in their conservation laboratory, thus offering a novel training opportunity to the developing profession.

In order to fill a growing need for broad-based training, the first graduate conservation training program in the United States was begun at New York University in 1960 (Conservation Center, Institute of Fine Arts, New York University, 14 E. 78th St., NY, NY 10021). It was followed in 1970 by the Buffalo Graduate Program in the Conservation of Historic and Artistic Works (Buffalo State College, 230 Rockwell Hall, 1300 Elmwood Avenue, Buffalo, N.Y. 14222) and in 1974 by the Winterthur Museum/University of Delaware Art Conservation Program (301 Old College, University of Delaware, Newark, DE 19711). Several other academic training programs now exist also; these usually have a specific focus, such as library and archival materials. Information on these can be obtained from the American Institute for Conservation.

Requirements for admission to these Masters degree programs include a Bachelor's degree with a significant course work in art history, chemistry, and studio art. Most programs also require experience as a technican or volunteer in a museum or conservation laboratory. The graduate programs generally include two years of courses in art techniques, materials science, methods of analysis, advanced chemistry, museum studies, conservation theory, and other related areas in addition to hands-on work in the laboratory. Each student chooses a major, usually paintings, textiles, paper, decorative objects, furniture, ethnographic and archaeological objects, or conservation science, although not all of the programs offer each of the majors. Generally, the third year is an internship in a conservation laboratory under the supervision of a professionally-respected conservator in the chosen area of specialization.

The great benefit of attendance at one of the programs is the condensation of information and opinions that might otherwise require a lifetime to obtain. Additionally, the training introduces the student to many different types of materials and objects. Immediately after graduation, the conservator is considered to be at an entry level to the profession and requires additional experience to supplement the intensive and broad background obtained in the program.

Each of the programs takes about 10 students a year, so competition for admission is keen. Since the demand for training is much greater than the programs can accommodate, many individuals choose instead to pursue a self-directed course of study consisting of a traditional apprenticeship supplemented with extensive readings and attendance at courses and conferences. It should be noted, however, that a Masters degree is becoming the expected standard of training, with many museums currently requiring the degree or equivalent in their advertisements of positions vacant.

As of this writing, only four conservators have graduated from the graduate programs with a specialty in furniture. Winterthur is the only program offering a furniture major, although Cooperstown allows object majors to concentrate in wood. Due to the inadequacy of training opportunities and the unfulfilled need for trained furniture conservators, the Smithsonian Insituttion has recently begun a certificate program (Furniture Conservation Training Program, CAL, MSC, Smithsonian Institution, Washington, DC 20560) which is designed to provide training in furniture conservation equivalent to that of a graduate program. It is organized as a part-time program that allows the attendees to maintain their current employment and other commitments for the first three years of training. Twelve two-week-long intensive courses are offered sequentially at three month intervals. After successful conclusion of the courses, the attendee completes a year-long internship under the supervision of a professionally-respected conservator. Extensive woodworking experience is required for admission. Additionally, the applicant must have a Bachelor's degree, two semesters each of general chemistry and art history, and a semester each of organic chemistry and drawing. The program accepts six students at the beginning of each three-year-long cycle of courses.

Furniture Conservation

The furniture conservation profession has developed only during the last few decades, much more recently than the conservation field as a whole. There are two primary reasons for this. The first is the relatively recent acceptance of furniture as important historic and artistic objects. This is currently reflected in the great increase in furniture prices, rivaling those of many paintings, although still behind the top prices obtained by paintings. Where only 20 years ago appearance was the most important factor in determining value and repairs were disguised, now original materials and workmanship are paramount and conservation treatments are intended to be detectable.

The second reason is the historically strong association of the craft of cabinetmaking with furniture repair. Remnants of the old guild system always have inhibited the sharing of information about treatment materials and techniques. In addition, when making new furniture with its smooth, even surfaces, cabinetmakers dictate their ideas to the wood. The use of utmost restraint necessary to treat an original, somewhat disfigured, historic object can be difficult for them. Thus, the tendency for over-restoration by making unnecessary replacements or improving the appearance of a piece is deeply rooted.

Additionally, cabinetmaking is only one facet of a multitude of skills and knowledge that form the essence of a conservator. An excellent cabinetmaker can be a poor furniture conservator, while an average cabinetmaker can be an excellent conservator. The key difference and the force that controls and directs a conservator's knowledge and skills is the all-important conservation attitude, which will be discussed in the next chapter on ethics of the profession.

Chapter 2

Furniture Conservation Ethics

In the first chapter, society's changing perception of historic furniture was examined. It progressed from viewing furniture strictly as useful tools to reflections of current style, then to chic representations of former style, and finally to the present view of historic furniture as aesthetically, historically, and culturally important documents. Corresponding with these developments were changes in attitude about repair. Early repairpersons were interested in making the piece of furniture once again functional. Appearance was probably secondary to use. Later, when furniture not only was useful but also handsome and represented current taste, repairs were intended to be both aesthetically acceptable and functional. Once historic furniture became in vogue, an appearance of age and undetectable or disguised repairs were important features, although functionality was also necessary. Current conservation attitude is much more complex, with intense respect for the integrity of the piece and its remaining original materials and evidence of workmanship, in addition to aesthetic and structural considerations.

AIC Code Of Ethics

With the development of the conservation profession as we know it today, the need became apparent for a document outlining conservation attitudes. This was undertaken by the American Group of the International Institute for Conservation, now the American Institute for Conservation, and was ratified in 1967. The AIC Code of Ethics and Standards of Practice is embraced by all conservation specialties, including furniture. This treatise represents and summarizes the conservation attitude which flavors every conservation activity and truly sets conservation aside as a unique profession. It is recommended that owners of furniture and wooden objects familarize themselves with the Code and use it to guide their dealings both with conservators and with the objects themselves (copies are available from AIC, 3545 Williamsburg Lane, NW, Washington, DC 20008).

The Code's Preamble nicely explains its entire concept:

Conservation of historic and artistic works is a pursuit requiring extensive training and special aptitudes. It places in the hands of the conservator cultural holdings which are of great value and historical significance. To be worthy of this special trust requires a high sense of moral responsibility. Whether in private practice or on the staff of an institution or regional center, the conservator has obligations not only to the historic and artistic works with which he is entrusted, but also to their owners or custodians, to

his colleagues and trainees, to his profession, to the public and to posterity. The following code expresses principles and practices which will guide the conservator in the ethical practice of his profession.

Integrity Of Object

Perhaps the most important aspect of conservation ethics is an intense respect for the integrity of the object, which influences all activities of a conservator, from recommendations for exhibition to proposed treatments. The original or historic character and components of a piece of furniture must be preserved whenever possible. It is important to distinguish between original appearance and original components, which many times exhibit the effects of age and use. Returning a piece to original appearance may necessitate destruction of important information about the materials and techniques used by the maker, in addition to obliterating cultural information about how the piece was used. If, for example, several pieces of veneer are missing from the edging of a top, minimum-sized replacement pieces should be set in, not the whole strip removed and a new one added. Removal of the entire strip, even if it is faster and makes the piece look better, results in loss of original material and is highly unethical, not to mention potentially devaluing. Along the same lines, sanding the wood before applying a new finish destroys the patina and color of the wood, removes the original surface, obliterates evidence of original production techniques and tool marks, reduces the original thickness and, therefore, is to be condemned.

Additionally, it should be noted that the original appearance is not necessarily the most important one. Alterations, both intentional or accidental, may have been made to the object that are important from a historic or cultural perspective. Examples include a sword slash on a table inflicted by Stonewall Jackson during the Civil War, wear on a chair rung indicating generations of supported feet, or alterations to a piece by the original maker a number of years after its manufacture.

An excellent example of this is the original wooden Wright Brothers' "Flyer" airplane (now in the National Air and Space Museum, Smithsonian Institution) which made the first powered manned flight in Kitty Hawk on December 17, 1903. After its flight that day, high winds blew the plane over and severely damaged it. The plane was shipped to Dayton, Ohio, and put into storage where, among other things, it was submerged by flood waters. In 1916, after receiving a request to exhibit the plane at the Massachusetts Institute of Technology, and again in 1925, Orville Wright repaired and restored the plane. It is known from existing records that certain original components were missing or severely damaged and therefore were replaced. These included the elevator and rudders, parts of the engine, and the fabric covering the wings. Orville's repairs themselves are important historic and cultural documents since they represent what the maker himself desired in his restoration.

Stable Materials

Another important element of conservation ethics is the use of materials and techniques that are stable and well-tested. It is important to know that a material will not deteriorate quickly and, more importantly, that treatment processes will not damage the object. Many pieces of furniture have been significantly harmed because an uninformed individual used a cleaner or varnish that slowly but steadily degraded the underlying surface. It is important to remember that such deterioration does not necessarily occur immediately, but over time its effects are compounded severely.

Retreatability

Additionally, every attempt must be made to use processes and materials that are reversible or removable, both immediately following use and after aging. This is critical for several reasons. Materials used in conservation treatments are subject to the same deteriorative processes as is the object. They will not last forever and the piece of furniture eventually will have to be retreated. Reversibility also provides for implementation of new and better treatments by allowing removal of the initial one without causing damage. Finally, there is always a chance something might go wrong during a treatment and reversibility insures being able to attempt it again. For these reasons, irreversible materials such as epoxies and drying oils generally are not used for conservation of wooden objects.

Documentation

Documentation of a piece's initial condition and record of treatment is another important ethical issue. Conservators produce a detailed treatment proposal prior to working on a piece and a treatment report after completion of the project listing the specific techniques and materials used. These written records are supplemented usually with a series of photographs taken both before and after treatment. The tools of X-radiography, infrared and ultraviolet photography, and various analytical procedures are used as necessary to provide further documentary information. Documentation allows present and future owners to know exactly what has been done to a piece of furniture and is especially helpful during future treatments or in the event of deterioration caused by previous treatments or improper care. It also prevents misrepresentation and confusion over what is original.

In a further attempt to clearly differentiate the work of the conservator from the historic components of the object, conservators will often choose to use materials and techniques that are easily detected as being modern. An extreme example of this would be the use of a Plexiglass pedestal to support a chair that is missing a leg. In many instances, this treatment option would be considered too aesthetically and functionally severe. A more generally acceptable approach would be to make a new leg of the same or similar species of new wood as the original with coloration as necessary to produce a harmonious overall appearance of the chair, not necessarily an exact color match. Areas that are not normally visible would not be colored, allowing easy detection of the new wood.

Value

In determining the proper treatment for a piece of furniture, the conservator must not consider the piece's value or aesthetic appeal. Each and every piece, regardless of age or rarity, deserves the same quality of treatment. In instances where funds are limited, the extent of the treatment can be adjusted, but never the quality. It therefore follows that a conservator can never answer the question of whether or not it is worth treating a piece of furniture. Besides being unethical to consider the piece's value, it is obviously a conflict of interest for the conservator since an affirmative answer will have a positive economic impact upon him/her. Only the owner can consider value when determining whether or not to proceed with a treatment. If the owner is uncertain of the piece's value, he/she should consult with a competent appraiser and not with the conservator. Bear in mind that value is not only economic, but also includes historic value, cultural value, and emotional value as well.

Uniqueness

Each and every piece of furniture is unique. These differences may be subtle but they are extremely critical. Even if two identical pieces are made at the same time by the same person, changes occur that are dependent upon the total environment and history of each piece. Obviously, each object is made of different pieces of wood, and even if they are from the same tree, they will have somewhat different properties. If the pieces of furniture have two different owners, the differing temperatures, relative humidities, and light levels in the two houses will cause differing degrees of deterioration. One owner may use a furniture polish, which will affect the nature of the finish, while the other does not. One piece may be subjected to daily spills, abrasion, and bangs while the other is used only for special occasions. Obviously, the piece receiving daily use/abuse will require more frequent repair and refinishing, probably with materials completely different from the original. Depending upon the abilities of the repairperson, it could even suffer severe damage to its integrity and character.

For these reasons, the conservator must consider the specific needs and condition of each piece of furniture in order to determine an appropriate treatment procedure. Coupled with the fact that there are usually several equally acceptable treatment options, it becomes obvious that a conservator must personally examine an object before giving a suggested treatment. It is impossible to approach conservation of furniture from the perspective of a definite and consistent "cookbook" solution for each conservation problem. This is precisely why a conservator must have such a broad background of training and experience.

Education

It is the conservators' responsibility to be aware of the latest information in their area of specialization in order to allow the best possible treatment of furniture in their care. Additionally, conservators have an obligation to the profession to share their knowledge with other conservators, including the training of students in both formal academic settings and as apprentices and assistants. Education of the public and other non-conservators is accomplished through publications, lectures, workshops, and the answering of public inquiries.

This chapter has presented a number of the key elements of the Code of Ethics as they apply to the conservation of wooden objects. Numerous specific guidelines and concepts are generated from the use of these standards. The knowledge and application of these are the essence of the conservation profession. The next few chapters in this series will discuss the basics of the technology of materials from which furniture is made in order to give the reader a better understanding of the major issues affecting deterioration and, therefore, preservation.

Chapter 3

Wood Technology

The first two chapters introduced the history of the profession and the ethical guidelines that define conservation. Since the major material composing furniture is wood, this chapter will examine the basic biological, chemical, and physical properties of wood, allowing the reader to understand better the underlying causes of furniture deterioration.

Misconceptions

We have all heard or read statements like the following. "Wood is alive and is constantly moving." "Wood needs to breathe." "As wood ages, it needs to be fed. This occurs as the wood consumes its natural supply of moisture and oils." These statements are blatantly incorrect and misleading. However, hundreds of books, articles, and advertisements contain similar mis-information and mis-advice. Part of the difficulty is the relatively great complexity of wood as a material. In the words of Bruce Hoadley, Professor of Wood Technology at the University of Massachusetts in Amherst, and author of the excellent book *Understanding Wood: A Craftsman's Guide to Wood Technology* (Taunton Press, 1980), "The biggest misconception is that somewhere there are 'experts' like me who know everything there is to know about wood" (*Fine Woodworking,* January/February, 1979, p. 81). Since the furniture conservation profession has emerged only recently, it is understandable that so many misconceptions still exist.

Cellular Structure

Trees are living plants and as such are organic material. They are composed of numerous types of specialized cells, most of which are many times longer than they are wide. Cells are of two general types, **longitudinal**, which run parallel to the stem or trunk of the tree and compose the vast majority of wood, and **rays**, which are perpendicular to the stem and radiate from its center to an outside edge (Figure 1). Wood cells in general have a cell wall and an inner cell cavity, appearing somewhat like drinking straws.

Figure 1

Vertical longitudinal cells running in the direction of the tree trunk are crossed by horizontal ray cells (magnified about 100 times).

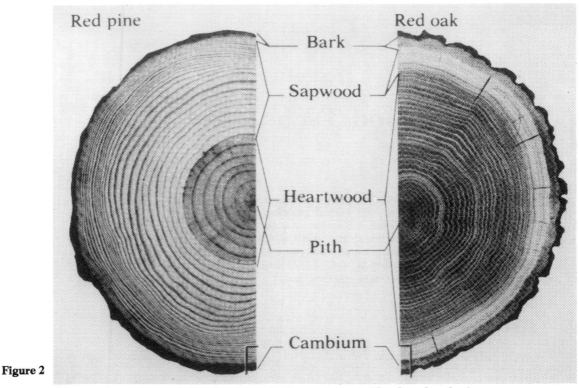

Figure 2

Cross-sections of a typical softwood, red pine, and a typical hardwood, red oak.

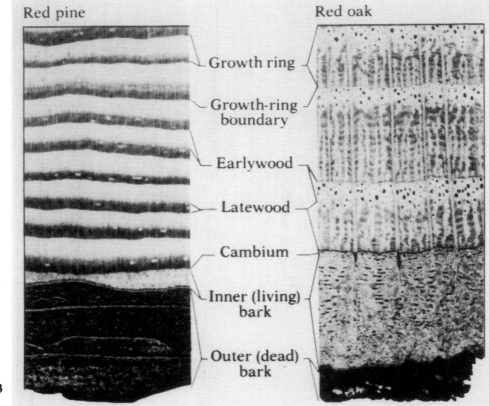

Figure 3

Enlargements of cross-sections showing early wood and latewood of red pine and red oak.

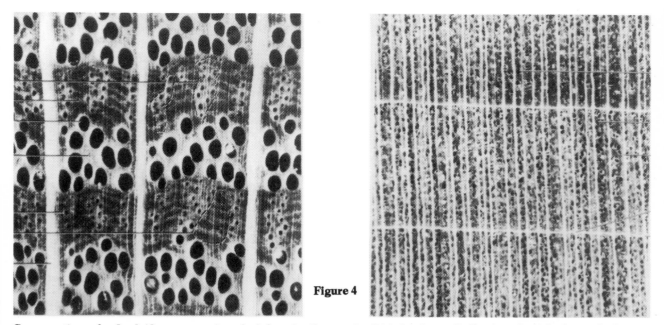

Figure 4

Cross-sections of red oak (Quercus spp.) on the left and yellow poplar (Liriodendron tulipifera) on the right (magnified about 10 times). Note that the oak pores are larger and more concentrated in the earlywood (ring porous). The poplar pores are smaller and scattered evenly in both earlywood and latewood (diffuse porous).

When one examines a cross-section of a tree, several features are visible (Figure 2). The **bark** on the outside protects the tree. Immediately beneath it is the **cambium**, a thin layer of living cells filled with protoplasm. These cell walls are very thin and fragile. As the cambium cells reproduce and divide, the inner cells undergo a change, losing living protoplasm and adding secondary walls of cellulose fortified with lignin. These newly-formed cells are **sapwood** and have walls which are rigid and impart strength. Sapwood cells conduct water and dissolved nutrients but most are **no longer alive**. About 10 percent of sapwood cells remain alive. As the tree grows and new sapwood cells are formed, the ends of the inner sapwood cells are sealed off, prohibiting the flow of fluids, and the cells become **heartwood**. The remaining living cells die and heartwood is **completely dead.** Compounds called **extractives** are formed and deposited in the heartwood cells, imparting the colors and decay resistance characteristic of different types of woods.

Growth in trees varies with the seasons (Figure 3). At the beginning of the growing season, wide diameter cells with thin walls are formed, called **earlywood.** Through the season, the cells become smaller with thicker walls, increasing in density and strength. These cells are termed **latewood.** The variation from earlywood to latewood on a cross-section creates the familiar pattern of growth rings.

Taxonomically, there are two groups of trees, the **gymnosperms** or **softwoods** and the **angiosperms** or **hardwoods.** Softwood cells consist mostly of tracheids, which provide support and fluid conduction and are about 100 times as long as they are wide, and a few resin canals running longitudinally, with the possibility of a few ray cells. Hardwood cells are more specialized, and longitudinal cells include tracheids, fibers, which provide strength, and vessels with open ends for conduction of fluids. Ray cells are generally more common and larger in hardwoods than in softwoods. When vessels are cut open during conversion of hardwood trees to boards, they are called **grain pores.** In some woods, such as oak, chestnut, and ash, the pores are concentra-ted in the earlywood and these woods are termed **ring-porous** (Figure 4). In other woods, the pores are scattered somewhat evenly, called **diffuse-porous.** In general, hardwoods are more dense, harder, and stronger than softwoods, but there are a number of exceptions to this.

Anisotropy

Wood is an **anisotropic** material, simply meaning that its properties are not uniform in all directions. This is caused primarily by the orientation of most wood cells along the direction of the axis of the tree and by the variety of types and sizes of cells. As a result, the three planes of wood, **cross-sectional, radial,** and **tangential** each exhibit different properties and appearances (Figure 5). All pieces of wood no matter how small exhibit all three planes.

Figure 5

The three planes of woods: tangential (T), radial (R), and cross-sectional (X).

The cross-sectional or transverse plane is perpendicular to the stem or axis of the tree. It appears as the familiar disk of wood with annual rings visible. Wood in the cross-sectional plane is often called **end grain** (Figure 2). The radial plane is parallel to the stem, passing through its center. Growth rings are perpendicular to the surface of the plane. The tangential plane is also parallel to the stem and is tangent to the growth rings (Figure 6). Boards cut from the radial plane are called **quarter sawn** and exhibit straight, parallel figure. Tangential boards, commonly called **flat sawn**, typically exhibit interlocked "U" or "V" figure, combined with wavy or straight figure (Figure 7). In reality, most boards are a combination of the radial and tangential planes and wood in these plans is commonly called **edge grain** and **side grain**.

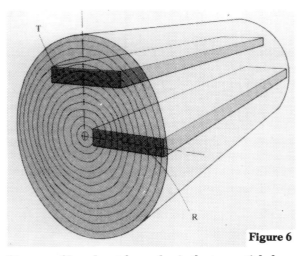

Figure 6

Diagram of boards cut from a log in the tangential plane (T) and the radial plane (R). Note the predominantly horizontal growth rings on the end of the tangential board and the vertical rings on the end of the radial board.

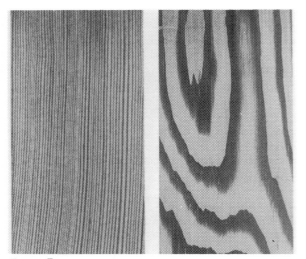

Figure 7

Radial plane boards (quarter-sawn) show straight, parallel figure and tangential plane boards (flat-sawn) exhibit wavy, often interlocked "V" figure, as illustrated by these two boards cut from the same larger piece of wood.

The three planes of wood play a role in wood identification. Each species of wood has different cellular characteristics, including cell type, size, shape, and location. To identify an unknown piece of wood, magnifications of the cross-sectional, radial, and tangential planes are examined and compared to known samples. Distinguishing between certain species can be extremely difficult, if not impossible, unless the sample size is quite large (such as the whole tree complete with leaves) or if extremely sophisticated techniques such as scanning electron microscopy are available.

Figure

The term **figure**, when applied to wood, refers to any variance from a plain surface. Thus masonite has no figure. However, technically, all boards have unique figure. Common types are grouped and given names (Figure 8). The appearance of figure is caused by variations of light reflectivity from the different sizes, shapes, angles, and colors of cells. Figure can normally be emphasized or deemphasized by the way the log is cut, as illustrated by the difference between the tangential and radial boards in Figure 7. Common types include **crotch**, formed where the trunk separates into a "Y"; **burl**, created in knob-like bulges on the trunk caused by abnormal and disoriented cell growth; **stump**, wood from the roots and base of the trunk; **rays**, revealed when quartersawing bisects the ray cells; **curl** or **tiger stripe**, which occurs when longitudinal cells grow in a wavy manner instead of straight; **bird's-eye**, produced by small swirls of abnormal cell growth; and **ribbon** or **stripe**, caused by the reflection of light from the alternating angles of cells from one growth ring to another, a phenomenon termed **interlocked grain**. Common in mahoganies, this last property makes the coloring of new wood during the treatment of a piece of furniture virtually impossible, since the color of the original wood changes with a change in the direction of lighting or viewing.

The strength of wood depends on many variables. Since wood is anisotropic, the plane from which the wood is cut affects its strength. Defects in wood, such

Common figure types: Figure 8

a) crotch in aspen,

b) burl,

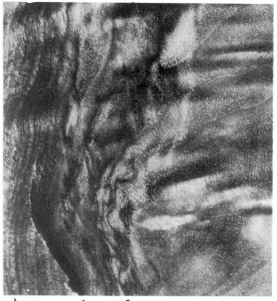

c) stump in walnut,

as knots, bark inclusions, horizontal growth, and abnormal cell growth, can weaken it. Contrary to popular conception, there is no difference in strength between sapwood and heartwood of a board. Generally, hardwoods, with the presence of fiber cells, are stronger than softwoods. The tensile strength (resistance to a pulling force) of wood in the longitudinal direction (along the grain) can be extremely high. Pound for pound, it can be greater than that of steel. However, the tensile strength perpendicular to the axis of the board (across the grain) is roughly 40 times less. It is precisely for this reason that most cracks in wood follow the grain.

A greater amount of cell wall material relative to the volume of cell cavities increases the density of wood. Generally, greater density implies greater strength and hardness. Hardwoods as a group are more dense than softwoods, although one of the least dense woods, balsa, and one of the most dense woods, lignum vitae, are both hardwoods. Wood is a reasonably flexible material and under the right conditions can be bent into varied shapes, as commonly illustrated by bentwood chairs.

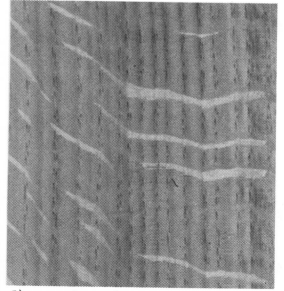

d) rays in oak,

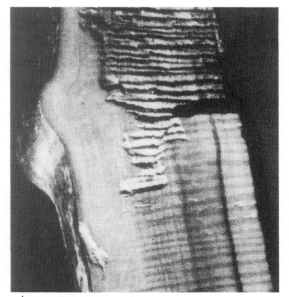

e) curl in maple,

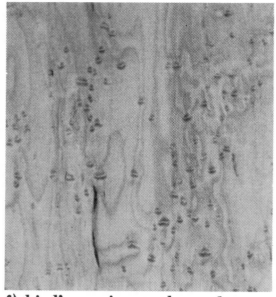

f) bird's-eye in maple, and

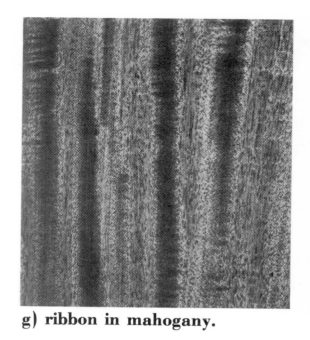

g) ribbon in mahogany.

Harvesting

Converting a tree into usable-sized lumber or veneer can be accomplished by a number of methods. One of the oldest of these is **riving**, which utilizes a froe and hammer to split logs into boards. This method is effective only on relatively short pieces of wood species that split easily, such as oak and cedar. The board surface follows the cells and therefore often is wavy and uneven (Figure 9). Riven boards usually have a triangular cross-section, since they are split from around a log.

Hand sawing produces boards that have saw marks at varying angles and spacings due to the variability of arm movement. Normally, the saw marks are not perpendicular to the axis of the log. Hand sawing was used commonly through the 18th century. **Up-and-down saws** are generally run by water wheels. The blade reciprocates in a vertical plane and as a result, the saw marks are perpendicular to the axis of the log and spaced about ¼ inch to ½ inch apart. Up-and-down saws were used through the early 19th century and much later in isolated areas. **Circular sawing** produces parallel arc-shaped cuts with a rapidly spinning blade often greater than 4 feet in diameter. It was invented around the mid-18th century but was not in common use until the early to mid-19th century. It is the most common sawing method used today. **Band sawing** utilizes a continuous loop blade running perpendicular to the axis of the log. Saw marks are straight, parallel, and about 1/16 inch to ⅛ inch apart. Common use of the band saw began around the mid-19th century.

Normally, boards were planed during the manufacture of furniture. This process removed the characteris-

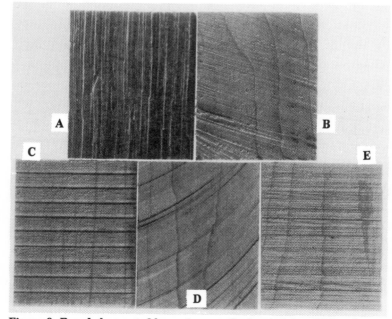

Figure 9. Boards harvested by various methods: a) riving, b) hand sawing, c) up-and-down sawing, d) circular sawing, and e) band sawing.

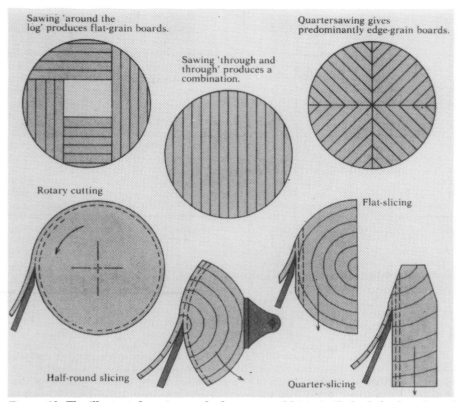

Sawing 'around the log' produces flat-grain boards.

Sawing 'through and through' produces a combination.

Quartersawing gives predominantly edge-grain boards.

Rotary cutting

Flat-slicing

Half-round slicing

Quarter-slicing

Figure 10. The illustrated sawing methods were used historically both for boards and veneer, while the cutting and slicing methods are more recent veneer harvesting methods.

tic marks created during the conversion of the trees to boards and veneers. Marks may still exist on undersides, insides, backs and other areas that are not normally visible, since cabinetmakers often saved labor by not planing boards in such locations.

Sawn veneer is cut from a log in a manner similar to boards. Sawing produces veneer that is thicker than other methods and can be cut from the radial or tangential planes to produce specific properties or appearances (Figure 10). This method wastes wood since the saw kerf destroys it. Historically, it was the only veneer harvesting method used until the 19th century. **Peeled** or **rotary cut** veneer is produced by mounting the log at the center of each end and rotating it against a fixed knife. This process results in an almost unlimited width of veneer sheets with primarily tangential grain figure. Plywood is typical of this method. **Sliced** veneer is produced when the mounted log is moved against a fixed knife in a straight or arced movement. This technique produces a combination of radial and tangential cuts of a width limited by the diameter of the log.

Moisture Equilibration

The **seasoning**, or **moisture equilibration**, of wood begins once a tree is cut and harvested (Figure 11). When the tree is alive, its cell cavities are mostly or completely filled with water, termed **free water**. The **moisture content (MC)** of wood is the weight of the water in the wood relative to the weight of the dehydrated wood (cell material), expressed as a percentage. The amount of moisture in a live tree can be quite large, often exceeding 75 percent moisture content, depending on the species of tree.

Seasoning begins with the evaporation of the free water from the cell cavities. Eventually, the cavities are

empty and only **bound water** remains in the wood, so called because it is chemically attached within the cell walls, causing them to be fully swollen (Figure 12). This condition of maximum bound water in the wood is called the **fiber saturation point (FSP)**. During this initial stage of seasoning, there has been no dimensional change of the wood as the free water has evaporated and the wood is commonly called **green**.

As the bound water begins to evaporate, the cell walls become less swollen, the cumulative effect of which causes the entire piece of wood to shrink. Evaporation of the bound water and its corresponding shrinkage continues until the amount of moisture (bound

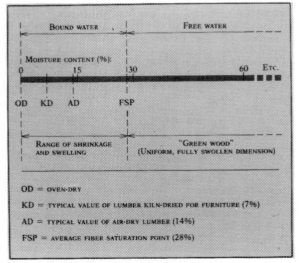

BOUND WATER		FREE WATER

MOISTURE CONTENT (%):

0   15   30   60   ETC.

OD   KD   AD   FSP

RANGE OF SHRINKAGE AND SWELLING

"GREEN WOOD" (UNIFORM, FULLY SWOLLEN DIMENSION)

OD = OVEN-DRY

KD = TYPICAL VALUE OF LUMBER KILN-DRIED FOR FURNITURE (7%)

AD = TYPICAL VALUE OF AIR-DRY LUMBER (14%)

FSP = AVERAGE FIBER SATURATION POINT (28%)

Figure 11. Wood moisture content values.

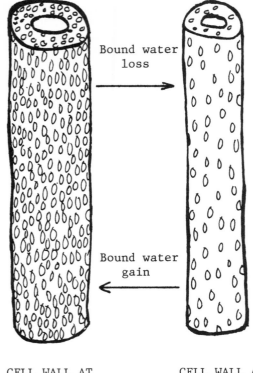

Bound water
loss

→

Bound water
gain

←

CELL WALL AT
HIGH
MOISTURE CONTENT

CELL WALL AT
LOW
MOISTURE CONTENT

Figure 12. Bound water molecules in the cell wall occupy space within the molecular structure. Loss of bound water from the walls allows them to contract, resulting in a smaller cell. Returning the cell to a high moisture content condition reintroduces bound water with resultant swelling. The cumulative effect of all the cells swelling or contracting causes dimensional change in a piece of wood.

Relative Humidity

The equilibrium moisture content of wood is controlled primarily by the relative humidity of the surrounding air. If the relative humidity rises, wood absorbs moisture, swelling the cell walls and expanding, eventually reaching a new equilibrium moisture content. If the RH decreases, wood cell walls give up moisture and contract, resulting in shrinkage of the piece of wood. This **hygroscopic** (water-attracting) process occurs regardless of the age of the wood.

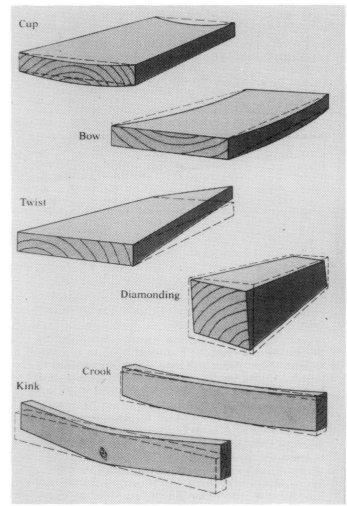

Figure 14. Types of warp in boards.

water) remaining in the wood is in equilibrium with the amount of moisture in the surrounding air, that is, with the **relative humidity (RH)**. This is called the **equilibrium moisture content (EMC)** of the wood at a given temperature and relative humidity. It is similar for all species of wood.

Figure 13. The left photograph shows red oak samples (longitudinal on top, radial in center, tangential on bottom) at their fiber saturation point, equivalent to 100 percent RH. The right photograph shows the same samples at 0 percent RH, equivalent to 0 percent moisture content. Note the amount of shrinkage in each sample.

A RH of 100 percent equals 25 to 35 percent equilibrium moisture content (depending on the species of wood) which is the fiber saturation point, and 0% RH equals 0% EMC, sometimes called **oven-dry**. A 100% RH change can cause an 8% or greater dimensional change in the tangential direction, 4% in the radial direction, and 1/10% in the longitudinal direction (Figure 13). For example, a 12 inch wide tangential board subjected to such a change would alter its width by an inch. As a convenient guideline to remember, a 10% RH change can result in roughly a 1% width change. In general, dimensional changes in the radial direction are about half this, and they are negligible in the longitudinal direction for wooden objects smaller than a house.

As wood seasons, it may distort or warp, normally caused by varying amounts of shrinkage from one part of the board to another (Figure 14). The amount of warpage depends on the cell configurations and variations and can be enhanced by defects in the board. It is often the result of the greater amount of shrinkage in the tangential direction than in the radial. Warp can also occur in boards that were at equilibrium moisture content and subjected to changes in moisture content. It is important to remember that most warps represent permanent distortions that can be removed only by applying severe stresses, with potential damage to the wood.

If a board attempts to expand and is restrained, the cells can become permanently squeezed together and crushed. When the moisture content returns to its original level, the board will be narrower. This permanent deformation is called **compression set** (Figure 15). Attempted shrinkage that is restrained will result in splits if the fairly low tensile strength of wood across the grain is exceeded. Shrinkage stresses are compounded if compression set occurred prior to shrinkage. Restraint is commonly caused by other parts of a composite object, including other boards. Restraint is worst if the grain direction of one board is perpendicular to that of another board to which it is attached.

The surface of wood reacts to RH changes first. The differential between the surface and the interior moisture contents sets up stresses that can cause distortion. This phenomenon can be demonstrated easily by wetting one side of a piece of veneer and noting the severe distortion (Figure 16). Large and rapid RH changes create the greater stresses. If the stresses are great enough, compression set or splits can occur on the surface of a board caused by the restraint of its own interior. This can result in permanent warpage (Figure 17).

Temperature

At a constant relative humidity, rising temperature causes a decreased moisture content and shrinkage, the result of the increased energy of heat driving off bound water from the cell walls. Falling temperature causes increased moisture content and expansion. The effect of temperature in the range commonly associated with historic objects is not nearly as great as that of relative humidity. As a general guideline, a 10 degree F change

Figure 15. An experiment to show compression set. All three samples were conditioned to about 35% relative humidity and attached at their bottom edges to a rigid frame. The righthand sample was not restrained or attached at its top. The center sample was restrained but not attached at its top. The lefthand sample was both restrained and attached at its top. The relative humidity was gradually raised to about 85% and returned to 35%. The righthand sample expanded freely and shrank back to its original size. The center sample, however, could not expand and was forced to undergo compression set. When the RH was returned to the original level, it was permanently smaller. The lefthand sample also underwent compression set. However, when it attempted to shrink as the RH returned to 35%, it was restrained by attachment at its top and bottom, resulting in tension great enough to cause a split at its weakest point.

Figure 16. Wetting one side of a piece of veneer causes the cells on that surface to swell, resulting in a curved profile. If compression set takes place, distortion can be permanent.

Figure 17. In addition to creating permanent cupping, repeated wetting of the surface of this board and not its underside caused splits or checking on the surface due to compression set.

will cause roughly a 1/6% change in tangential width (compared to a 1% width change for a 10% RH change). Higher temperatures cause more rapid chemical reactions, including oxidation of wood, resulting in faster darkening of its surface. Temperatures above about 180 degrees F can cause the beginning of the breakdown of the cellular structure of wood and temperatures over 451 degrees F result in its combustion.

Light

Light is a form of energy and will permanently bleach the natural colorants (extractives) in wood (Figure 18). In higher interior light levels, bleaching can occur surprisingly rapidly, especially if the light source is high in **ultraviolet (UV)** light. These high energy wavelengths of light are just outside of the blue end of the visible light spectrum and are present in significant quantities in daylight and fluroresecent light. Additionally, ultraviolet light will destroy portions of the cellular structure of wood. Indoors, normally, cell destruction is fairly slow and effects the surface and the cells immediately beneath it.

Biopredation

Wood is subject to biopredation by both animals and plants. Termites, carpenter bees and ants, powder post beetle larvae, and other insects can severely deteriorate wood by eating channels beneath the surface. Fungal infestation will occur only near the fiber saturation point when the RH is around 100 percent or when an external moisture source is available. Molds and mildew can grow on the surface of wood and may stain it, but usually will not cause serious damage. Other fungi, however, can completely destroy wood. Deterioration by both animals and plants will be discussed in more detail in a later chapter.

This chapter has surveyed the aspects of the technology of wood that are pertinent to furniture deterioration and preservation. The next chapter will examine the nature of finishes and adhesives, two extremely important but often overlooked components of furniture.

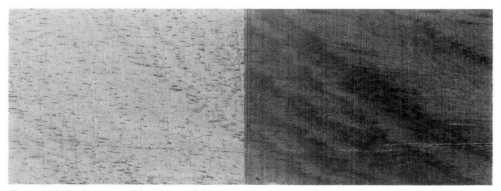

Figure 18. Light causes bleaching of the natural colorants of wood, as in this sample of Cocobolo, a species of rosewood.

Chapter 4

Technology of Adhesives and Finishes

At this point in the booklet, the reader should have a basic understanding of the nature of wood. The first part of this chapter will examine one of the least visible but most important parts of furniture — the adhesives that hold it together. It will begin with an examination of general adhesive theory, followed by the types and properties of historic and modern adhesives. The second part of the chapter similarly will investigate finishes that have been used on furniture.

Adhesives

Materials being adhered to one another are called **adherends** or **substrates** (Figure 1A). In furniture, the adherends are usually wood to itself or another component material such as brass, ivory, mother of pearl, leather, or gesso. Not surprisingly, the material actually attaching the adherends is termed an **adhesive** and the attraction of the adhesive for the substrate is called **adhesion.**

The mechanism for adhesion requires that the adhesive, after setting, must have a strong attraction for the adherends. In addition, it must have strong **cohesion** or attraction for itself. An adhesive bond will fail when either the adhesive or the cohesive strength is exceeded or if the tensile strength of the substrate itself is exceeded. Therefore, the least strong component of the system limits the bond strength. In general, the smaller the space between the adherends (the tighter the joint), the stronger the adhesive bond. This is because the cohesive strength of most wood adhesives in a thick layer is usually lower than the cohesive strength of the wood or other adherend, thus weakening the overall bond strength. Large gaps are caused by substrates that are not smooth and even or by inadequate pressure during bonding.

The three basic types of adhesive setting mechanisms are **solvent evaporation**, exemplified by liquid hide glues or white glues (polyvinyl acetate emulsions), **thermosetting** as found with hot melts, and **chemical reaction,** such as epoxies and super glues (cyanoacrylates). Adhesives that set by solvent evaporation are characterized by shrinkage as the adhesive dries. If the

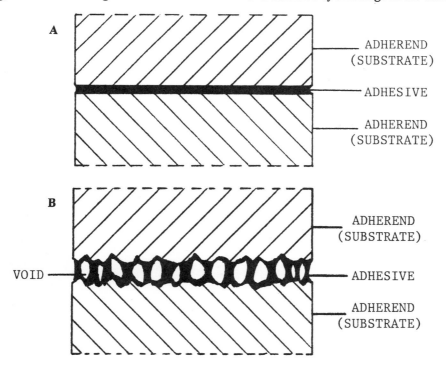

Figure 1. A) Idealized adhesive joint with smooth adherend surfaces and a continuous, uniform adhesive layer. B) Adhesive joint typical of solvent-based adhesives used for furniture. Adherend surfaces are uneven, causing a relatively large gap between them. As the adhesive dried, it shrank, resulting in voids in the adhesive and a weakened joint.

bond gap is large, adhesive setting results in significant voids in the adhesive and a weakened bond (Figure 1B). Pure solvent setting adhesives are reversible, although aging can alter this property. Thermosetting adhesives normally have minimal shrinkage and are therefore good gap fillers. They usually are reversible with heating and with solvents. Chemically setting adhesives generally do not shrink and are also good gap fillers. However, since they react to become chemically different materials when they set, they are difficult, if not impossible, to reverse. Additionally, by their nature, many are less stable and are prone to more rapid deterioration than other types of adhesives. Many adhesives combine more than one setting mechanism and as such have properties that are characteristic of a combination of setting types.

As a general rule, wood adhesives are brittle and inflexible, although there are some exceptions to this, such as hot melts and rubber-based adhesives. Most are not able to flex enough to compensate for the potentially large dimensional change of wood in an uncontrolled environment, therefore resulting in bond failure.

Since the primary adhesive used on furniture through the early 20th century was hot hide glue, it would be helpful to examine its use and application. Hot hide glue is a protein adhesive refined from the skins, tendons, and hooves of various animals. It thermosets initially to a gel as it cools and completes its setting by water evaporation.

The gluing process begins as the wood surfaces are prepared and the joints are cut. A tight fit is necessary for a strong joint, as hot hide glue has very low cohesive strength in thick layers. The surfaces to be adhered are cleaned of dust and dirt. The glue is prepared by mixing dry flakes in water and heating in a double boiler. It is brushed quickly on both surfaces and the wood pieces aligned and clamped before it sets to a gel. The open time before setting can be extended by heating the components or by applying heated blocks to the joint after assembly. The excess squeezeout is removed with a dampened cloth. After drying, usually overnight, the clamps are removed.

There are many variables for error and a weakened joint. These include an incomplete spread of glue due to the short open time, a thick glue line because of rapid gelling or inadequate pressure, joint movement after setting has begun, or using old or overheated glue. It is not surprising, therefore, that many hot hide glue joints have failed.

For conservation purposes, the ethical principles of reversibility and long term stability severely limit the number of adhesives that can be used. The major ones are hot hide glue, liquid hide glue (basically the same material as hot hide with an ingredient added to allow it to remain liquid at room temperature), some polyvinylacetate emulsions (white and yellow glues), and occasional use of hot melts. There is still a great need for research into the appropriateness for conservation use of many different adhesives.

Finishes

The three major functions of a finish are to moderate the interaction of moisture with wood, to provide an aesthetically pleasing appearance, and to protect against damage to the wood from use. In addition to conventional transparent finish coatings, the term finish also includes paint, gold and other metal leafs, and miscellaneous surface treatments.

Finishes slow diffusion of moisture into and out of wood, helping to prevent damage from relative humidity changes. To be completely effective, the finish must be applied evenly to all wood surfaces, including undersides, insides, and backs. Otherwise, uneven moisture content change caused by fluctuating relative humidity can cause warpage and possibly compression set or splits. Figure 2 shows typical summer to winter changes in moisture content of unfinished wood in an interior heated environment without relative humidity control. The application of a finish to all surfaces mode-

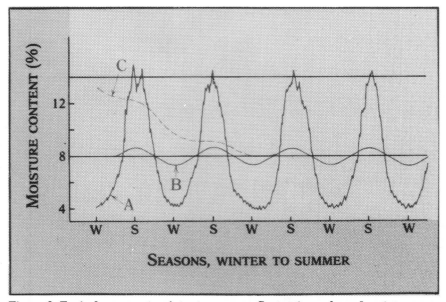

Figure 2. Typical summer to winter to summer fluctuations of wood moisture content caused by uncontrolled interior relative humidity in the temperate United States. The moisture content changes are accompanied by dimensional changes of the wood. (From Understanding Wood **by Bruce Hoadley. Used with permission of the Taunton Press, Inc. C 1980 The Taunton Press, Inc. All rights reserved.)**

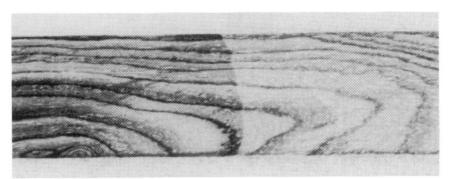

Figure 3. The left-hand side of this board has been coated with a finish, increasing the wood's color saturation and appearance of depth.

rates the moisture content changes to the sine wave in the center of the figure (marked with the letter B). There is a great range in the effectiveness of different finish materials as vapor barriers and, therefore, a great variance in moderation effectiveness. Additionally, a thicker layer of a finish is a better vapor barrier than a thinner layer of the same finish.

It should be noted that even an ideally-applied finish will not prevent moisture content change and the resulting dimensional change of the wood. It simply increases the amount of time necessary for this to occur. Additionally, historic furniture usually is not finished on all surfaces like the ideal example and, therefore, less protection is afforded from damage caused by relative humidity changes.

Aesthetically, transparent finishes enhance the grain pattern and saturate the wood colors (Figure 3). This is achieved by producing a smooth surface that scatters less light than the raw wood, thereby increasing color saturation. In general, the thinner and more even the finish, the more attractive the wood appears. Additionally, different types of finish materials have differing appearances and aesthetic appeal.

Protection from use is provided by finishes in several ways. Since finishes predominantly are on the surface of the wood, they will receive abrasion before the wood surface is reached. Obviously, if the abrasion is great enough, the wood will be damaged as the finish is penetrated fully. Finishes also can protect from spills, fingerprints, dirt, and pollutants. They are much easier to clean than the raw wood itself.

Common finish application methods are by rag, brush, spray, and French polishing. This latter technique involves a pad, called a rubber, into which is put a little dilute shellac. The rubber is constantly moved over the surface, in essence depositing hundreds of extremely thin coats. French polishing requires extensive practice and even the most experienced polishers occasionally experience difficulties in achieving the desired appearance due to the great number of variables, including concentration of shellac, pad movement, dust, relative humidity, and rate of application.

Most application methods require that the finish material(s) be dissolved in a solvent to render them the proper consistency for application and leveling before they harden by evaporation of the solvent. Some finishes harden additionally by chemical reaction with oxygen in the air (called polymerization or, more specifically, crosslinking) and are thus no longer reversible in the original solvent. This is particularly true of oils and oil-based varnishes, and of modern polyurethanes. Other modern finishes set by a polymerization reaction

begun when their two parts are mixed together, similar to the setting process of epoxies.

Gloss control of finishes can be done during application by the addition of inclusions such as cotton linter, metal soaps or silica, or by the use of a fast or a slow drying solvent. After drying, gloss can be affected by abrasion with sandpaper, steel wool, pumice, rottenstone, or other polishing compounds. High gloss results in greater wood color saturation and an appearance of depth. This is the result of more light being reflected from the wood surface to the eye of the viewer. Matting or dulling a finish causes scattering of light and thus a reduction of color saturation and depth.

Examination of cabinetmakers' recipe books of the 18th and early 19th centuries indicates a wide variety of materials were used for finishing and coloring. There is much discussion in these manuals of methods for obtaining high gloss finishes, contradicting the 20th century mythology of a preference for flat or mellow finishes.

The general types of materials mentioned in the recipe books include waxes, commonly beeswax; natural resins and gums such as dammer, sandarac, rosin, copal, and gum mastic; and oils including linseed, poppyseed, and walnut. Often several different materials were combined in the same finish. Shellac, refined from the exudate of the lac bug in Southeast Asia, did not come into prominence in the western world until the late 18th to early 19th centuries. It was extremely common through the 19th and early 20th centuries, when its use was reduced greatly after the introduction of synthetic finish materials.

Colorants added to finishes were essentially the same as those used for textiles and included materials such as alkanet root, dragon's blood, logwood, Brazilwood, cochineal, indigo, and verdigris. Most colorants were added to the finish, not the wood itself. Normally, color was applied directly to the wood only for chairs, although inlays were sometimes dyed completely through before application.

Contrary to the rather frequent claims by some dealers, very few pieces exist with original transparent finishes intact. Of the few that have managed to survive the stripper's lairs, virtually all have been adulterated with innumerable types of polishing and cleaning materials and truly can not be called original.

Twentieth century finishes include synthetic waxes refined from petroleum products (microcrystalline), chemically modified oil-based varnishes, lacquers (nitrocellulose and acrylic), and chemically reactive two-part finishes.

For conservation treatments, by far the most common finish material is shellac. Waxes often are used on top of existing finishes. As more conservation research is completed, materials such as specific types of acrylic resins are gaining popularity.

Paint

The three basic components of a paint are the pigments, medium, and vehicle. **Pigments** impart color and opacity to paints. They are finely ground powders that originally were natural earths and currently include synthetic materials. The **medium** binds the pigment particles together and to the surface when the paint has dried. Common mediums include oil (oil paints), egg (tempera), casein (milk paint), acrylic resin (acrylic paints), and other materials, including various varnishes. The **vehicle** is the solvent used to dissolve the medium and produce a workable paint consistency.

Generally, paint is applied directly on the wood surface of furniture, although it may be applied over gesso (a chalk or whiting and gelatin mixture) or varnish.

Lack of adequate flexibility of paints on wood is a common problem, resulting in cleavage, flaking, and loss of paint.

Metal Leaf

Metal leaf, extremely thin sheets of nearly pure metal, commonly gold or silver, is normally applied over a gesso ground, although occasionally leaf will be applied as a highlight over varnish or paint. Often, a thin layer of bole (extremely fine clay mixed with dilute gelatin) is applied over the gesso prior to the laying of the leaf. Gesso is very brittle and is the victim of severe cleavage and loss when applied over wood substrates that are not in a controlled environment. Because of its thinness, metal leaf is very easily damaged by abrasion and even regular cleaning can cause complete loss.

At this point in the booklet, the reader should have a good understanding of the nature of the major materials composing furniture. The next chapter will examine how these materials are interrelated in furniture construction.

Chapter 5

Furniture Construction Techniques

Composite Object

The preceding chapters have presented a background on the properties of some of the materials of which furniture is made. This chapter will examine how materials are interrelated and attached to one another, which introduces a key concept for all of furniture care and conservation — a piece of furniture is a **composite** object. It consists of a number of different materials, each with its own specific properties and each reacting in its own unique way to environmental influences. The overall sum of the nature and properties of the composite materials make up the individual character of a piece of furniture.

Joinery

The primary interaction of materials in a piece of furniture is that of the wooden components with one another, without which furniture as it is known today would not exist. The cutting and working of wood to facilitate its attachment to other components is termed **joinery**. Joint strength depends on a combination of the physical interlocking of wood parts, adhesive strength, and/or the mechanical strength of fasteners, such as nails or screws. In examinig different joint types, note that end grain (cross-sectional plane) adhesion does not add appreciably to joint strength. Side grain adhe-

sion (radial and tangential planes), however, is potentially as great as the strength of the wood.

There are only four orientations of wood grain that are possible in joinery, **end grain to end grain, side grain to end grain, parallel side grain to side grain**, and **perpendicular side grain to side grain** (Figure 1). Every type of wood joint is composed of one or more of these four orientations. In examining joints, bear in mind that wood movement caused by changes in moisture content is about twice as great in the tangential direction as it is in the radial direction, and is negligible in the longitudinal direction.

This effectively means that a board is rigid along the grain and moves significantly across the grain. Additionally, different species of wood will change dimensions differently in response to the same moisture content change. Recall that wood movement can result in compression or tension set, splits, and adhesive failure.

End grain to end grain orientation produces a very weak adhesive joint, although wood movement is likely to be somewhat complementary since the boards will contract and expand in the same direction, but not necessarily the same amount (as one may be radial and the other tangential).

Side grain to end grain results in a fairly weak adhesive joint also caused by poor end grain adhesion.

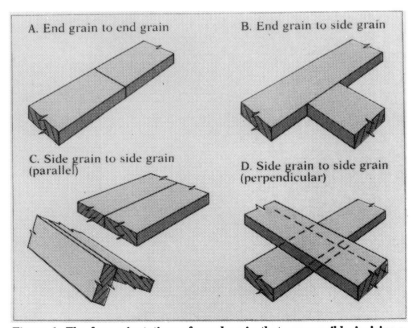

Figure 1: The four orientations of wood grain that are possibly in joinery. (From Understanding Wood **by Bruce Hoadley. Used with permission of the Taunton Press, Inc. c. 1980 The Taunton Press, Inc. All rights reserved.)**

Wood movement is likely to be contradictory due to the perpendicular orientation of the boards.

Parallel side grain to side grain allows excellent adhesion. Movement of wood is normally complementary. However, radial and tangential boards attached to one another may move different amounts, as may boards of different species. This is the strongest possible joint orientation for adhesion and is the least likely to suffer deterioration caused by wood movement.

Perpendicular side grain to side grain, called **cross-grain** construction, also facilitates excellent adhesion but movement of wood is contradictory, possibly over-stressing the adhesive or the wood. Only if the moisture content of the wood is constant (constant relative humidity and temperature) is this joint equally as strong and stable as parallel side grain to side grain.

At this point, the major types of joints will be surveyed quickly. Be cognizant of the amount of physical interlocking of wood, as opposed to the need for an adhesive or fastener. Also note whether side grain from the radial or tangential planes (excellent adhesion), or end grain from the cross-sectional plane (poor adhesion) is involved. Look for potential problems that may arise from wood movement caused by contradictory wood orientation (side grain to end grain or perpendicular side grain to side grain).

A **butt** joint has no physical interlocking of the wood. Its strength depends entirely on an adhesive or mechanical fastener. Butt joints commonly are used to edge join boards to form wider stock (Figure 2).

A **mitre** joint does not have physical interlocking of wood and also depends upon adhesives or fasteners for strength. The combination of end and side grain weakens an adhesive bond. Mitre joints can be reinforced with splines and dowels. They often are used for picture frames and where corners of moldings meet (Figure 3).

Figure 2: Butt joints open and assembled. The two on top are end grain to side grain and the lower two are parallel side grain to side grain.

Figure 3: Mitre joint open and assembled.

The **lap** joint has some physical interlocking, but usually requires an adhesive or fastener. Common uses include x-shaped bases and supports for tables (figure 4).

Figure 4: Lap joint open and assembled.

Historically, the **mortise and tenon** joint was the primary joint used by **joiners** for **framed** construction. The hole cut in one member is the mortise and the tongue on the other is the tenon. It has good mechanical interlocking in all but the direction in which it is assembled and as a result must be glued or mechanically fastened with a pin to prevent it from pulling apart. This joint commonly is used for framed door panels and the joining of seat rails into the legs of chairs, in addition to many other applications. Mortise and tenon joints can be round or rectangular (Figure 5).

A **dado** is actually a variation of the mortise and tenon. The entire end of the board is the tenon. The joint commonly is used for attaching drawer supports to sides of cases and for stiles between drawers (Figure 6).

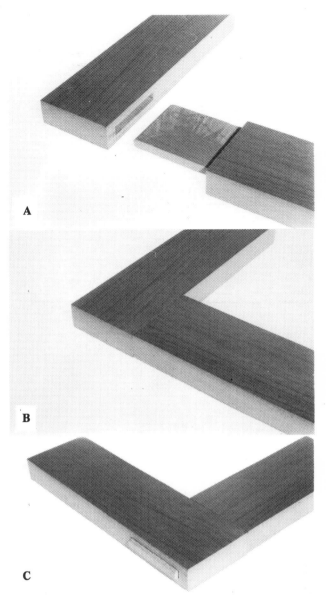

A

B

C

Figure 5: Mortise and tenon joint open and assembled. This specific joint is a through tenon since the tenon protrudes completely through the wood member that contains the mortise, visible in C. Through tenons can be slit and small wedges of wood driven into the openings to help lock the joint in place, as was common in Philadelphia-area mid-18th century chairs where the seat rails join the rear legs.

Figure 6: Dado joint open and assembled.

Figure 7: Tongue and groove joint open and assembled.

Figure 8: Spline joint open and assembled.

The **tongue and groove** also is related to the mortise and tenon, with the joint running along the entire long edge of the board. It normally is used to provide some mechanical interlocking when joining narrow boards into wide surfaces without the use of adhesives, such as backs and bottoms of chests (Figure 7).

The **spline** joint is actually a tongue and groove with a removable tongue (the spline) and it often is used to align two pieces of wood in adhesive applications, as well as to strengthen glue joints that have a lot of end grain, such as mitres (Figure 8).

A **rabbet** joint can be viewed as a mortise that is missing one mortise side and is open. It often is found where drawer bottoms attach, where the backs of pieces join the cases, and on the backs of picture frames. Mechanical fasteners are common with this joint (Figure 9).

Figure 9: Rabbet joint open and assembled.

The **dovetail** joint revolutionized woodworking by allowing case construction and the profession of cabinetmaking to develop. Surprisingly, it was known to the ancient Egyptians but disappeared and was re-discovered in late-Medieval Europe, reaching America in the late-17th century. It consists of wedge-shaped tenons, called pins, cut on one piece and corresponding wedge-shaped mortises, defining tails, on the other. Occasionally, especially on Germanic pieces, the dovetail pin is split and wedged, locking it in place without the need for a fastener, which ordinarily is an adhesive. The dovetail is used extensively to attach ends of boards to one another, such as drawer sides to fronts, chest sides to tops, and, in a sliding manner, to attach the legs to the columns of tripod tilt-top tea tables and the rails between drawers to the sides of chest of drawer cases (Figure 10).

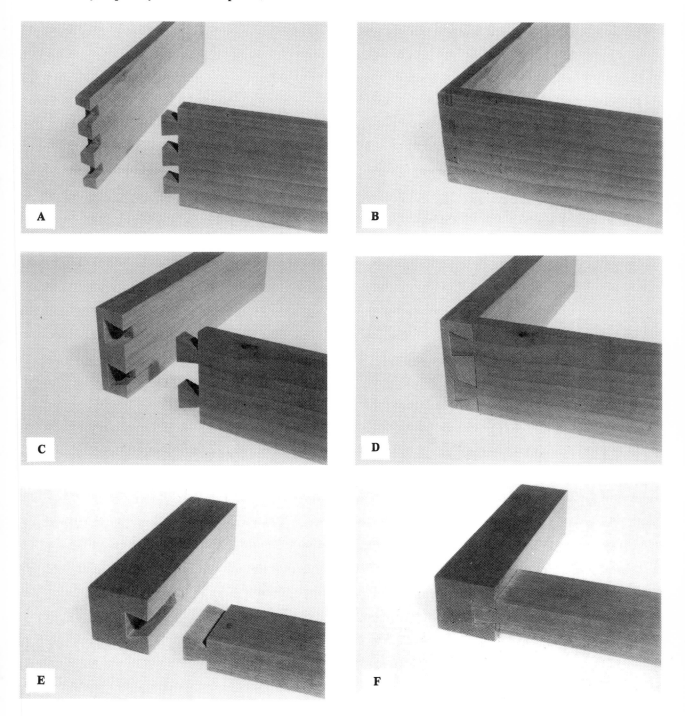

Figure 10: Dovetail joints open and assembled. A and B are a through dovetail. C and D are a half-blind dovetail. The saw cuts on the inside of the lefthand board are created by overcutting the joint to allow easier removal of the waste wood. E and F are a sliding dovetail.

The **dowel** joint is essentially a mortise and tenon with a removable round tenon and round mortises in both wood members. In general, dowel joints are weaker than an equivalent mortise and tenon joint. Dowels came into widespread use in the mid-19th century because the joints could be made easily by machine and, as a result, they are the predominant joint found in Victorian furniture (Figure 11).

Many types of specialty joints exist, most of which are a combination of more basic joint types. Different areas of the world and regions within a country may have used their own peculiar types of joints (Figure 12).

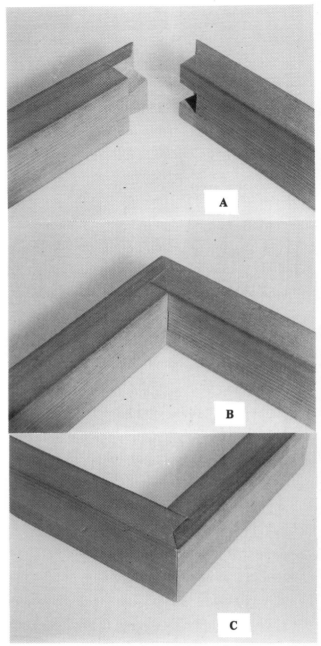

Figure 12: Mitre-blind-dovetail joint. A is open. B is assembled viewed from the inside. C is assembled viewed from the outside.

Figure 11: Dowel joint open and assembled.

Figure 13: Veneer on secondary wood.

Veneering

Veneering is a joinery method that merits an in-depth examination. Veneer attachment to the support wood is actually a butt joint, depending entirely on the strength of an adhesive. The surface area of the glue joint is huge compared to the size of the veneer, resulting in a very strong joint if the adhesive is applied properly (Figure 13).

However, an extremely important factor in the overall strength of the veneering joint is the nature of the support wood, called **secondary wood, substrate** or **ground work.** Since secondary wood of a piece of furniture usually is not visible, furniture makers could use many varieties of materials, construction techniques, and qualities of workmanship (Figure 14). Poor con-

A

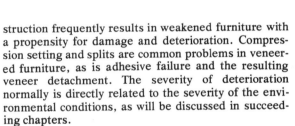

B

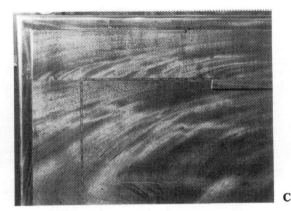

C

D

Figure 14: The veneered side of the panel (A) gives no clue to the nature of the secondary wood (B). Similarly, the corner of a Roentgen-attributed table, circa 1795, (C) is veneered on both sides and the secondary wood is not visible. Examination of an X-radiograph of the same corner (D) shows the secondary wood structure to be quite complex. It consists of an outer frame with a cross member mortise and tenoned into it at the bottom left. The center of the rectangle formed by these members is filled with small wood rectangles that are oriented at 90 degrees from each other like a checker board. The outside of the small rectangles are held to the surrounding frame with spline joints.

struction frequently results in weakened furniture with a propensity for damage and deterioration. Compression setting and splits are common problems in veneered furniture, as is adhesive failure and the resulting veneer detachment. The severity of deterioration normally is directly related to the severity of the environmental conditions, as will be discussed in succeeding chapters.

Marquetry (designs created by the use of various species and colors of woods) and **Boulle** (marquetry using tortoise shell and brass, silver, or pewter) are two

Figure 15: Marquetry designs, such as this late-19th century example, can be quite complex.

Figure 16: Cutting marquetry with a fret saw and extremely fine saw blades. Note the paper pattern glued on the top of the stack of materials.

specialized veneer construction techniques. The surfaces created using these processes can be quite complex, with an amazing variety of pattern, color and perspective (Figure 15). The designs often are made by stacking thin sheets of each material needed for the design with a sheet of paper between each one. The layers are glued together with hide glue and the pattern glued on top. The design is then cut apart following the pattern with an extremely thin saw blade and the sandwiches of individual parts removed from the rest of the design (Figure 16).

Each of these stacks is separated into the individual identical elements. This guarantees that the correctly-shaped piece of one material will fit in the same-shaped hole in another. Thus the design can be constructed by choosing the desired elements, assembling them as a unit, and gluing the whole pattern at once to the secondary wood. It is obvious that additional variations of the same pattern can be made by utilizing the remaining cut-out pieces (the total number of variations is equal to the number of layers of materials used originally). Marquetry can also be done by cutting out individual elements, placing them on the background wood, marking around them, cutting away wood within the mark to produce a cavity, and gluing the piece in place. Objects made with marquetry and Boulle techniques have the same general properties and deteriorative propensities as other veneered objects, although the combination of many different parts and materials often causes them to be more fragile.

Fasteners

Virtually all joints require some kind of fastener to keep them from pulling apart. This becomes apparent when one considers the fact that the joint must slide together when the cabinetmaker assembles the piece and, therefore, the wood components can be slid apart in the reverse direction unless held with a fastener.

Friction of wood to wood is usually not adequately strong to keep a joint together, particularly if compounded by the potential loosening effect of compression set, as discussed previously. Other common fasteners include nails, screws, hinges, and pegs.

Pegs are held in place by friction against the surrounding wood, which is enhanced by compression as they are driven home. Adhesives can be used to increase their holding power. Pegs are used most frequently with mortise and tenon joints. After the joint is assembled, a hole is drilled through the front side of the mortise, the tenon, and into the rear side. The slightly oversize wooden peg then is driven into the hole, effectively locking the joint in place. For this reason, pegged mortise and tenon joints can be assembled without adhesives, although often one is used. Some mortise and tenon joints utilize a peg hole in the tenon that is drilled offset from the hole in the mortise. When the peg is driven home, the joint is drawn together tightly. Pegs can also be used to attach drawer bottoms to sides and moldings to cases. Common peg shapes include round, square, and "lemon," a shape used frequently by Germanic craftsmen (Figure 17).

Nails also gain their holding power from friction. As a nail is driven in place, the wood fibers are compressed and bent, creating resistance to the withdrawal of the nail. Early nails were hand wrought and uneven in their shaft shape and length and in their head profiles. This type of nail is commonly called rose-headed and the shank tapers in profile from thickest at the head to a point (which is sometimes flattened) at the opposite end, in essence being an extended cone. Developments in the later 18th century in machine production technology allowed the manufacture of cut nails by a stamping process. This greatly reduced the cost of nail production and resulted in nails whose shanks were square or rectangular in profile and were flat on two sides and tapered on the remaining two from thickest at the head

Figure 17: Open and assembled pegged mortise and tenon joint.

to thinner at the blunt point. In the mid-19th century, the process of making modern wire nails was developed and the cost of nails fell even further. Early wire nails look essentially the same as the nails currently available in hardware stores, with a round even diameter cylindrical shaft and an abruptly tapered point (Figure 18).

Screws depend also on friction to hold securely, although the principle of leverage created by their threads gives them much greater holding power. Early screw threads were cut by hand, resulting in somewhat uneven spacing between threads. Additionally, the sides of the shafts of early screws are basically parallel and the ends are blunt. If one examines them carefully near the head, the shafts will show indentations in the metal where they were held with pincers while the threads and slot in the head (which is often off-center) were being cut. Modern machine-made screws were commonly available by the mid to late 19th century. They have a tapered shaft and a sharp gimlet point (Figure 19).

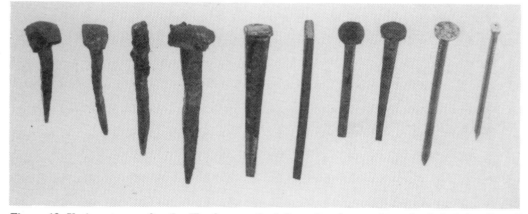

Figure 18: Various types of nails. The four on the left are hand wrought on both their heads and shanks. The next four to the right are stamped and the two on the right are modern wire nails.

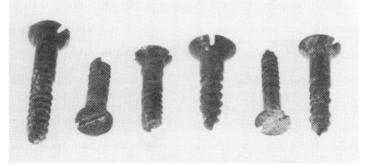

Figure 19: Types of screws. The left three screws are hand made. Note the essentially straight shafts, the blunt ends and the off-center slot in the head of the second screw from the left. The three screws on the right are modern machine-made screws with tapering shafts and a sharp point.

Hardware

In addition to the fasteners previously mentioned, furniture commonly incorporates hardware of various types. Metal hinges are used to attach leaves to tables, locks are found inside desk lids, and pulls allow the opening of drawers. Each of these items has an important function and contributes to the overall appearance of the piece of furniture. Additionally, hardware can be subject to deterioration itself and can even create problems for the wood and surrounding materials.

Finishing

Once a new piece of furniture has been jointed and assembled, it is ready for finishing. The surfaces are smoothed, historically with scrapers and more recently with progressively finer grits of sandpaper. The smoother the wood, the more attractive will be the final finished result, as any scratches or unevennesses are amplified by the finish.

Recall that a finish serves three primary purposes: to be aesthetically pleasing through optical saturation of the colors of the wood; to protect from use; and to provide a barrier to rapid moisture content changes of the wood that result in dimensional change. Normally, the aesthetic function of a finish demands primary attention and, as a result, numerous materials and application techniques can be used to produce a wide variety of results. In general, a finish is applied in a solvent, historically by brush, rag or French polishing and in the 20th century by spray, in one to twenty coats. The newly-applied liquid finish flows and levels itself before the solvent evaporates and the solid finish material is left behind. The success of the leveling depends upon a number of factors, including the dilution of the finish, the evenness of the surface, the application method, and the skills of the applicator. Maximum aesthetic results are achieved with thin, extremely even finishes. Therefore, cabinetmakers interested in the best finish will use many coats of very dilute finish with light abrasion after each coat has dried.

This chapter has discussed how materials can be combined to make a piece of furniture. The overall interaction of all of the components — wood, adhesives, surface decoration, finishes, fasteners, hardware — determines the amount of stability or deterioration a piece of furniture will exhibit when it is subjected to a specific environment. The next chapter will begin to examine these environmental factors and their effects on furniture.

Chapter 6

Furniture Deterioration:
Temperature and Relative Humidity

The preceding chapters have built a foundation of understanding of the furniture conservation profession, the chemical and physical properties of materials from which furniture is made, and the ways in which these materials can be combined to make a piece of furniture. The remaining chapters in this booklet will examine the specific effects of the environment on deterioration of furniture, and what the owner can do to minimize these effects.

The environment of a piece of furniture includes not only the natural conditions of temperature, relative humidity, light, airborne matter, and biological entities, but also the human factors of usage, original design and construction, care and repair. This chapter will examine the two natural conditions that cause the greatest amount of deterioration — temperature and relative humidity.

Temperature and Relative Humidity

Temperature and relative humidity (RH) are intimately related, as an examination of the meaning of the term relative humidity will explain. Air, like wood, has the capacity to absorb moisture vapor. However, it can hold only a certain maximum amount, dependent upon its temperature (Figure 1). The warmer the air, the more moisture it can hold before becoming saturated. Excess moisture is given off as dew, or in extreme cases as rain. The **relative humidity** of air **at a specific temperature** is the absolute amount of moisture vapor in the air at that time (called **absolute humidity**) divided by (relative to) the maximum amount of moisture the air can hold **at that temperature**. Relative humidity is expressed as a percentage.

Examination of Figure 1 shows that air at 70 degrees Fahrenheit can hold a maximum of 8 grains/cubic foot of moisture. If, on a particular day, 70 degree air has 4 grains/cubic foot of moisture, it has a relative humidity of 50 percent (4 divided by 8). If, on a different day, air of 70 degrees has 6 grains of moisture, its relative humidity is 75 percent (6 divided by 8). Let us assume that during this day, the temperature rises to 80 degrees, and no additional moisture is added to the air. The maximum amount of moisture the air can hold at 80 degrees is 12 grains/cubic foot. Thus the air now has a relative humidity of 50 percent (6 divided by 12), instead of the original 75 percent at 70 degrees.

A similar scenario occurs within a building during the heating season. Assume the outside air is 20 degrees and 100 percent RH (2 grains/cubic foot of moisture). It is heated to provide an interior temperature of 70 degrees and no additional moisture is added (no humidification). The interior relative humidity will be 25 percent (2 divided by 8). If the outside air has a lower RH, say 50 percent, the interior will have an even lower relative humidity of 12.5 percent (1 divided by 8). The relative humidity will be lower also if the outside air is colder or

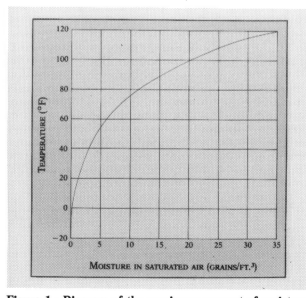

Figure 1 - **Diagram of the maximum amount of moisture air can hold at different temperatures, as indicated by the curved line. Air at a given temperature can hold less moisture than the line indicates, but never more. From** Understanding Wood **by Bruce Hoadley. Used with permission of the Taunton Press, Inc. c. 1980 The Taunton Press, Inc. All rights reserved.**

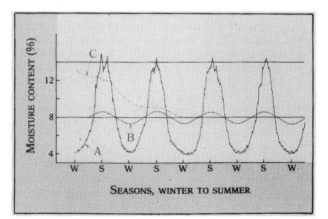

Figure 2 - **The jagged peaks of this diagram indicate typical fluctuations of moisture content of wood from the lows of winter to the highs of summer. This is caused by relative humidity variations. From** Understanding Wood **by Bruce Hoadley. Used with permission of the Taunton Press, Inc. c. 1980 The Taunton Press, Inc. All rights reserved.**

if the interior is kept at a higher temperature. Interior winter relative humidities of 5 to 20 percent are extremely common in areas with moderate to severe winter temperatures, such as most of the United States and Canada.

During the summer, interior air will be the same relative humidity as exterior air if environmental systems (air conditioning or dehumidifiers) are not used. This creates commonly an interior relative humidity level that is between 60 and 100 percent. Thus, a cycle from low RH in the winter to high in the summer is created (Figure 2).

Deterioration

How does this fluctuation affect furniture? Wood absorbs moisture from the air and expands when the RH goes up, and gives off moisture and contracts when it goes down (Figure 3). Additionally, rising tempera-

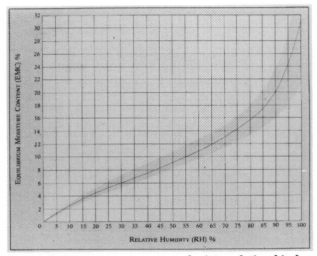

Figure 3 - **This curve represents the interrelationship between equilibrium moisture content of wood and relative humidity. Changes in moisture content result in changes in dimension of the wood. From** Understanding Wood **by Bruce Hoadley. Used with permission of the Taunton Press, Inc. c. 1980 The Taunton Press, Inc. All rights reserved.**

ture causes a decrease in moisture content and contraction of wood, and falling temperature results in an increase in moisture content and expansion. Since a piece of furniture is a composite object of different types and sizes of wood, joined by various methods, and utilizing particular adhesives, finishes, and other components, a number of problems can occur. It must be stressed that each piece of furniture is unique in its reaction to deteriorative forces, and specific damage can be predicted only generally. For this reason, examination of basic types of deterioration is desirable.

Veneer is very thin and must be supported by secondary wood, to which it is glued. It is, therefore, forced to respond to dimensional changes of the secondary wood. If cross-grain construction is used, stresses are compounded. Hide glue, the most common adhesive used until the 20th century, can be brittle, particularly when it has aged or at low relative humidities. Thus, adhesive failure is pervasive. Adding to the precarious existence of veneer is the fact that, since it is on the surface, it will be affected first by RH and temperature changes. The interior secondary wood which has not yet reacted to the change acts as a rigid material, causing the veneer to undergo compression set.

For the preceding reasons, it is extremely common to find veneer splits and detachment. Many loosened, protruding pieces subsequently are torn away and lost (Figures 4, 5).

Boards are subject also to compression setting and splits when they are restrained in a piece of furniture. Failure will occur at the weakest part of the board, often a glue joint if one is present. Common examples are splits in the sides of chests of drawers due to cross-grain attachment of the tops, bottoms, moldings, metal hardware or of the drawer supports inside the case,

Figure 4 - **The cracks in this veneer crossbanding were created when the surface veneer tried to respond dimensionally to relative humidity changes but was prevented from doing so by the secondary wood to which it was glued. The adhesive was eventually overstressed and failed, resulting in veneer losses.**

Figure 5 - **In this example, the secondary wood responded dimensionally to relative humidity changes, forcing the veneer, some of which was glued to it cross-grain, to buckle and detach. Additionally, the secondary wood split vertically, forcing the veneer to do so as well.**

splits in panels rigidly fixed in a mortise and tenon frame (the same panel allowed to float in the frame would not have split), and the cracks in fall-front desk lids caused by the attachment of cross-grain battens at the ends (Figures, 6A, 6B, 7, 8, 9).

Different types of joints suffer characteristic deterioration due to fluctuating relative humidity and temperature. The tenon in a mortise and tenon joint can undergo compression set caused by restraint of the mortise, resulting in a loose joint, or possibly a split tenon or mortise cheek. Additionally, mortise and tenon joints used to attach crossgrain members to boards will cause restraint of the board and result in its splitting (Figures 10, 11, 12).

Figure 8 - Had this raised panel been free to float in its frame, the split would not have occurred. Often, misguided restorations result in such panels being glued in place.

Figure 6A - The bottom of this box separated at a glue joint since its movement was restrained by nails to the box side.

Figure 6B - The bottom of a desk and bookcase split along the wood grain due to restraint by the sides and attached moldings.

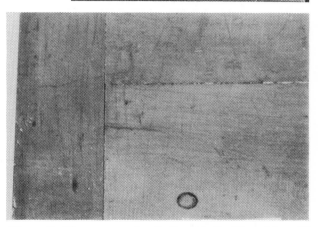

Figure 9 - The cross-grain attachment of a "bread-board" end restrained the movement of the horizontal boards of this desk lid causing the visible splits.

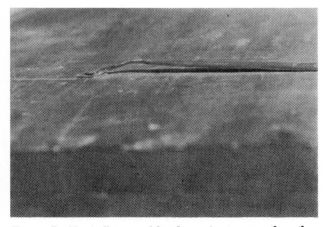

Figure 7 - Normally, metal hardware is stronger than the wood and inflicts damage on it when the wood tries to move. In this example, the back of the blanket chest bent the strap hinge when the wood contracted.

Figure 10 - The end-molding of the top of this blanket chest is attached by through tenons, effectively preventing movement of the top. The split and detached molding are the result. Also visible is the smaller tenon created by compression setting against the edges of the mortise.

Dovetail joints are usually parallel construction and therefore are less subject to damage than other construction types. However, two boards joined in this manner may not respond the same amount or at the same rate, depending, among other factors, on whether they are radial or tangential. The result can be joint loosening caused by compression setting and splitting of the boards (Figure 13).

Mitre joints will open at their corners when subjected to moisture content change due to temperature and relative humidity fluctuations. Increased moisture content (expansion) results in an opening at the outside of the joint. Decreased moisture content (contraction)

Figure 11 - The mortise and tenon of this chair was pinned. Resulting dimensional movement of the leg split the side of the mortise. Once looseness occurred, stresses from use accelerated the damage.

Figure 13 - Compression setting and wood movement loosened these dovetails. Also, compression setting of the exterior surface of the box back caused it to warp, further separating the dovetails.

causes opening at the inside corner of a mitre and possible compression setting. Fluctuations, therefore, can cause permanent openings in mitre joints, a phenomenon that is common with picture and mirror frames (Figure 14).

Dowel joints are subject to many of the same problems as mortise and tenon joints. Dowels commonly suffer compression set, which is more severe in their tangential direction due to greater dimensional movement in that plane. Joint looseness and weakening re-

Figure 12 - The headboard is tenoned into the post of this bed. When it tried to respond dimensionally to relative humidity changes, splits occurred. Note that the tenon itself split at the bottom of the figure.

Figure 14 - Typical mitred-corner separation. Note that the gap is largest at the inside and the outside corners are still touching. This would indicate that the moisture content of the frame when this picture was taken was lower than its moisture content when it was made or that it had suffered compression set.

sulting from the failure of the adhesive holding the dowels to both wood members is very common.

In addition to splits, compression set and adhesive failure, moisture content change can create warpage of wooden components of furniture. Warpage occurs when the exposed surface of a board reacts to a temperature or relative humidity change and the interior and other side have not yet reacted. This response can create compression setting of the surface wood cells. When the moisture content returns to the original level, the exposed surface of the board, which is now permanently smaller, will exert tension on the whole board, pulling it into a distorted shape (Figure 13).

Initially, one might find fault with cabinetmakers for not allowing in their designs and construction tech-

Figure 17 - Cleavage and loss of paint from a bed footboard.

niques for expansion and contraction of the wood. However, the ability to control tightly the interior temperature of a building (with the resulting vast RH swings from summer to winter) is a relatively modern development. Drafty 18th century winter interiors were quite cold. Heat was concentrated near the fireplace or stoves. As a result, the interior relative humidity was much higher in the winter, probably rarely dropping below 50 percent, compared to the common contemporary level of less than 20 percent. Since their interior environments were naturally more stable than ours, historic cabinetmakers did not have to deal with problems that were as severe as those we have today. On the other hand, modern cabinetmakers should be aware of current environmental fluctuations and accordingly design and build their furniture to minimize damage.

Figure 15 - Finish crazing. Note the generally parallel lines primarily oriented perpendicularly to the grain direction.

Figure 16 - Severe cracking of a finish. This is approaching a condition commonly termed "alligatoring." In this example, light probably contributed to the damage caused by wood movement.

Figure 18 - The finish opacity in this example results from detachment of the finish from the wood. It is a form of cleavage that has not yet flaked away.

Damage from cycling temperature and relative humidity is not limited to the wood itself. Many finishes (gilt, other metal leaf, and painted finishes in addition to transparent finishes), especially those that have embrittled with age, are not able to flex enough to accommodate wood movement. Lack of adequate flexibility results in **crazing** (fine fracturing), **cracking** (more severe fracturing), and **cleavage** (fracturing combined with lifting and detachment from the wood) of the finish. The visible effects of such deterioration are decrease of gloss, visual unevenness, loss of transparency, and, in severe cases, yellowish or whitish opacity and finish loss. Needless to say, all of these forms of deterioration lead to a shorter finish lifespan (Figures 15, 16, 17, 18).

Temperature, in addition to its effect on wood moisture content and relative humidity, also has an effect on deterioration rates. Higher temperatures promote faster chemical reactions and, thus, greater deterioration of all types of materials, but especially of finishes and adhesives. As a rough rule of thumb, a 10 degree Centigrade (18 degree Fahrenheit) rise causes a doubling of reaction speeds. Thus deterioration proceeds twice as fast at 88 degrees F as it does at 70 degrees F.

Stabilization Levels

It should be clear from the above discussion that in order to maximize preservation, one must stabilize the temperature and the relative humidity. An absolutely constant level of both is best, although the specific figure chosen will depend upon the naturally occurring exterior conditions. For most areas of the United States, recommended levels are 50 percent RH and 70 degrees F. These figures represent a level that is a comfortable temperature for human occupation and is a relative humidity compromise between the highs of the summer and the interior lows of the winter. Thus, the suggested levels are easiest to maintain year-round.

If it is not possible to maintain absolutely constant conditions, limit the amount of fluctuation. A fluctuation from 45 to 55 percent RH is safer than 40 to 60 percent, which in turn is safer than 30 to 70 percent. A similar relationship exists for temperature. Bear in mind that the greater the temperature or relative humidity variation and the faster it occurs, the greater the potential for damage. Gradual changes are safer for objects, especially for those with finishes or veneer.

It should be noted that buildings themselves also may be subject to accelerated deterioration due to increased winter relative humidity levels. The likelihood of this occurring depends on the exterior temperatures, the building age, construction and condition, the interior temperatures and RH levels, and various other factors. The mechanism of deterioration involves condensation of water in the outside walls and ceilings as interior moisture diffuses through them and is cooled. This water can freeze, causing expansion damage, or, in warmer weather, it can cause rotting of wood. Low exterior and high interior temperatures and relative humidities promote building deterioration. For this reason, some experts recommend that in cold areas such as Canada and the northern United States, the interior relative humidity at 70 degrees F should be held at 35 percent in the winter, instead of the generally recommended level of 50 percent. This setting should minimize building deterioration but may cause additional damage to wooden objects as described above. An effective, continuous vapor barrier on the inside (warm side) of walls and ceilings that are exposed to the cold may prevent all or most of this migration of moisture.

In areas with specific climatic differences, such as the Southwest's low relative humidity environment, the recommended relative humidity levels may not be the best. If, for example, a piece of furniture was made in Arizona, it will naturally have a low moisture content corresponding to the low ambient relative humidity (assuming the cabinetmaker used seasoned wood). Regardless of whether the furniture remains in Arizona or is shipped somewhere else, say Philadelphia, it would be best kept at a constant low relative humidity, perhaps 25 percent. If it were placed in a higher RH environment, the wood would expand and undergo compression setting and possibly splitting. On the other hand, if a piece was made in Philadelphia, it would be best kept in a 50 percent environment regardless of whether it was displayed in Philadelphia or Arizona. Shipping such a piece to the Southwest and placing it in dry ambient conditions would cause wood contraction and splitting. This phenomenon is observed frequently when furniture is imported from Europe or Asia where it has been in a naturally high RH climate. Soon after arriving in the United States, splits, distortion and detachment of parts occur as the furniture equilibrates to its new lower RH environment.

If it is necessary to change the ambient relative humidity from the level to which a piece of furniture has become equilibrated, it should be done very slowly. The change should take place over several months, if possible. Longer times allow less severe stresses as the components of the piece of furniture change dimensionally in response to the RH change.

Measurement

Now that the merits of a constant environment are evident, how is control accomplished? The first consid-

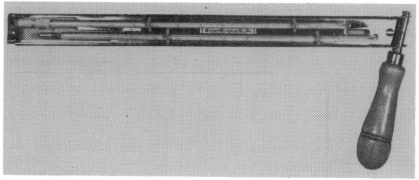

Figure 19 - Sling psychrometer.

eration is monitoring of the existing environment. If one does not know the current conditions, it is impossible to design a method of controlling them. A number of devices exist for this purpose. The thermometer is well known for temperature measurement and needs no discussion. A **sling psychrometer** measures both temperature and relative humidity (Figure 19). It is based on the principle that moisture evaporates faster in drier environments, thus creating a greater cooling effect. Two thermometers are held in a case next to one another. A wick on one is wetted, and the unit twirled in the air to speed evaporation. After about a minute, the dry temperature (ambient) and the depressed wet temperature are read and recorded. Reference to a chart determines the RH based upon the temperature depression differential. Sling psychrometers are very accurate and reasonably priced. **Battery-driven motorized psychrometers** work on the same principle as the sling (Figure 20). Instead of being twirled, though, a

Figure 20 - Battery psychrometer.

small battery-operated fan pulls the air over the wetted wick. They are very accurate as well and higher priced. **Digital hygrometers** rely on electronic circuitry to produce a relative humidity reading (Figure 21). They are portable and give a rapid response but are rather expensive.

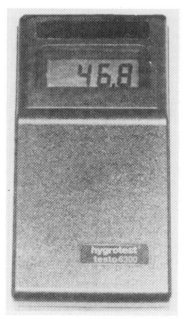

Figure 21 - Digital hygrometer.

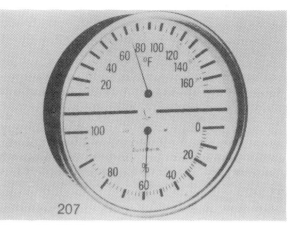

Figure 22 - Dial hygrometer.

Dial Hygrometers can be read directly, but vary greatly in quality, accuracy, and price (Figure 22). In general, more expensive units are more accurate than cheap units, which are virtually useless. Dial hygrometers are normally placed in one location and not moved from room to room due to their slow response time. All dial hygrometers should be checked periodically with a psychrometer or digital hygrometer to ensure accuracy. Inexpensive units which are not adjustable must be discarded when they read inaccurately. **Strip indicators** consist of small squares of salt-saturated paper. They turn from pink to blue as the relative humidity changes. By comparing the colors to a standard, the RH can be estimated to about 10 percent accuracy. They are cheap and give a broad approximation of the RH.

Recording hygrothermographs create a continuous week-long record of temperature and relative humidity on a paper chart (Figures 23A, 23B). Their clock mechanism must be wound and the chart changed once a week. Calibration is required at intervals and their cost is high, but they are convenient and accurate. They are the primary measurement and recording method that should be considered by museums and serious collectors, as they provide a continuous record 24-hours a day, allowing the detection of virtually all fluctuations.

When an environment is monitored, each separate area must be individually measured, ideally on a daily basis. In a house, normally, this requires checking individual rooms unless the floor plan is open, allowing good air circulation. Written records of all the readings should be kept (in the absence of a recording hygrothermograph). This will allow the detection and correction of fluctuation trends, be they seasonal or weekly.

Control

Most interior spaces are already equipped to control temperature through the use of the heating/air conditioning systems. Therefore, specific temperature control suggestions will not be made. Lowering the relative humidity is generally necessary during the summer or if a space is below ground. **Air conditioners** remove some moisture from the air as they cool it. Under certain conditions, they may be adequate. Obviously, they are completely ineffective when the outside temperature approaches or drops below that of the interior. **Dehumidifiers** condense moisture from the air. Many portable units must be manually emptied, but central systems can be tied directly to a drain. **Raising the temperature** will cause the RH to drop. However, this method is effective only when temperatures are below the desired interior level, such as in basements or in unheated buildings during the winter.

Generally, it is necessary to raise the relative humidity during the heating season. **Humidifiers** add moisture to the air. Portable units must be filled frequently with water, while central systems can be connected directly to a water source. A humidistat (similar in operation for RH control to a thermostat for temperature) can be installed with central systems that allows automatic maintenance of a desired relative humidity. However, they must be checked manually on a regular basis to ascertain accuracy. **Lowering the temperature** raises the RH. This method is particularly useful for unoccupied buildings (where maintenance of temperature for human comfort is not necessary). Regardless of the humidification system used, **furniture must be kept away from heat sources.** Air at these locations is hottest and, therefore, driest, with the greatest potential for damage.

With any of the above control methods, the critical ingredient is monitoring. The best and most sophisticated system will damage furniture if it is not properly set and maintained. It can not be assumed that automatic controls are accurate. The degree of owner involvement will vary from frequent, with simple and therefore less expensive techniques, to occasional, with automated systems. The choice between time, economics, and personal comfort is one each owner will have to make individually.

This chapter has examined two of the most severe deteriorative forces on furniture — temperature and relative humidity. The following chapter will discuss three others — light, environmental contaminants, and biopredation.

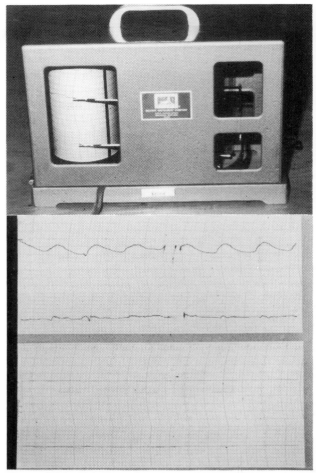

Figure 23A, B - Recording hygrothermograph and two weekly charts. The upper chart shows tremendous daily temperature and relative humidity swings which are certain to cause damage. The lower chart is close to ideal readings.

Chapter 7

Furniture Deterioration: Light, Environmental Contaminants and Biopredation

As discussed in the preceding chapter, temperature and relative humidity fluctuations cause more deterioration of furniture than any other natural environmental agent. However, light, contaminants and biopredation also can cause severe damage to — and even total destruction of — wooden objects.

Light

Light is a form of energy in the electromagnetic energy spectrum (Figure 1). The amount of energy contained by different types of radiation increases as the wavelength becomes shorter. Thus, energy increases from radio waves to infrared (IR) to visible light to ultraviolet (UV) to X-rays. Detailed examination of the visible light spectrum, that region of the electromagnetic spectrum that the human eye can detect (Figure 2), shows infrared radiation bordering the low energy end and ultraviolet radiation, the high energy end. Within the visible spectrum, energy levels increase from red through orange, yellow, green, and blue to violet. Daylight contains the entire visible light spectrum, as well as IR and UV radiation.

When visible light or UV radiation strikes an object, the molecules on the surface of the object become more energetic, causing certain deteriorative processes to occur. If IR radiation is present, the surface is heated, accelerating all types of deterioration. Indoors, damage is limited normally to the finish layers and the top one or two millimeters of the wood surface. Finishes can become embrittled and crazed. More advanced deterioration can result in pronounced cracking of the finish and may culminate in crumbling and total finish loss (Figure 3). Visual manifestations of light damage to finishes are loss of gloss, decreased optical saturation of the wood colors, and increased finish opacity. Wood itself suffers from loss of its natural colorants, resulting in a lightened appearance (Figure 4), and from the destruction of portions of its cellular structure, making it

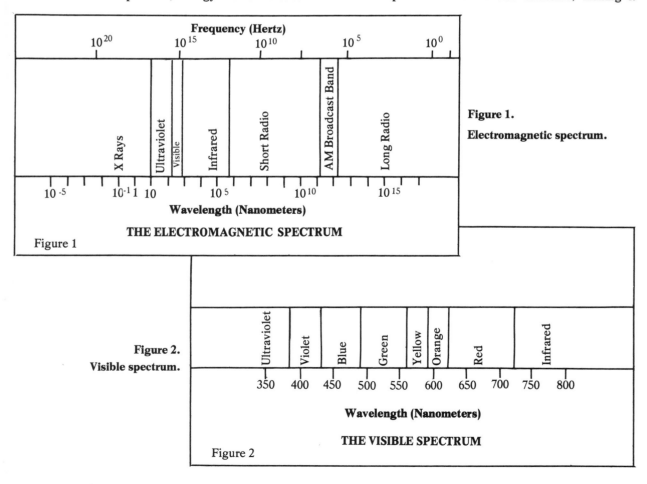

Figure 1.

Electromagnetic spectrum.

Figure 2.

Visible spectrum.

Figure 3. The finish that was protected beneath a glass knob is in excellent condition, while the area that was exposed to light is severely crazed and cracked, with crumbling and loss visible in the upper right of the figure.

Figure 5. The desk was displayed for 10 hours a day for a number of years with an electrified candlestick on its top. The area not protected by the candlestick was bleached.

weaker and prone to abrasive loss. Textile (upholstery) and paper components of furniture are extremely sensitive to light damage and can be bleached and weakened very quickly.

The amount of degradation caused by light is directly proportional to the energy level of the light, its intensity and the duration of exposure. Thus, the greatest amount of deterioration is caused by ultraviolet and blue radiation that is very bright and present for long times. This occurs when direct sunlight shines on furniture for much of the day. Indirect daylight is less intense than direct sunlight, but still contains high-energy radiation. Most fluorescent lighting contains a high proportion of ultraviolet radiation and blue light and is, therefore, more damaging than an equal exposure of incandescent light, which contains more lower energy red light and IR radiation. However, even low levels of incandescent lighting can create damage if exposure times are long enough (Figure 5).

To minimize damage, therefore, it is necessary to reduce light intensity levels as far as possible, filter the most harmful wavelengths of radiation, and limit to a short time the length of exposure. The ideal situation is constant darkness, although usually this is not practical. Light intensity can be reduced simply by drawing curtains, shutters and shades. Alternatively, objects can be moved out of the rooms that are the brightest.

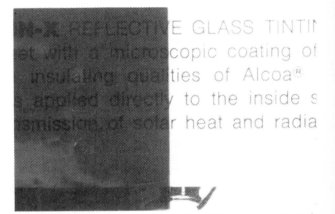

Figure 6. Light intensity reducing film covers the left portion of the figure.

Light intensity reducing films are available that can be applied to windows to cut the amount of light transmitted through them by as much as 90 percent (Figure 6). Intensity of artificial lights can be reduced by using lower wattage bulbs or fewer bulbs.

Ultraviolet radiation and some of the blue light can be filtered from light entering a building. It is important to realize, however, that the greater the amount of blue light removed, the yellower the appearance of the remaining light; therefore, under most circumstances,

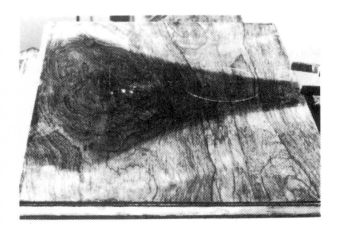

Figure 4. The center of the rosewood veneered top was protected from light damage by a triangular-shaped sculpture which was displayed on it.

Figure 7. UV absorbing sleeve for fluorescent bulbs.

only a portion of the blue light can be filtered without raising aesthetic objections. Filtering films can be applied to windows in a manner similar to intensity reducing films. Similarly, certain varnishes that incorporate absorbing agents can be painted onto window glass. Also available are filtering rigid plastic sheets, such as Plexiglass, that can be installed over existing glazing or added to the inside of windows, serving a dual function as interior storm windows. Plastic UV absorbing sleeves may be fitted over fluorescent bulbs (Figure 7). UV and light filtering materials absorb radiation, converting it to heat which is dissipated. Therefore, the effectiveness of the absorbing properties may be slowly reduced and the filtering materials may have to be replaced eventually. The length of time necessary for this to occur depends upon the specific nature of the absorbent material and the exposure conditions, but may be as long as several decades. Measurement devices are available to detect the intensity of both UV and visible light. These allow determination of the effectiveness of older filtering materials as well as measurement of the actual radiation levels in a room.

Exposure time can be reduced by drawing shades and curtains for as long as possible. Lights, especially fluorescents, should be turned off when not absolutely necessary. This is especially critical for furniture stored in areas that are used infrequently. For such pieces, covering them with soft cloth, such as unbleached muslin, will reduce significantly light intensity and exposure time (Figure 8).

Figure 8. Covering pieces with soft cloth will reduce damage from both light and dirt.

Contaminants

The air that circulates around wooden objects contains two primary types of contaminants that pose a threat to their stability: corrosive chemicals and dirt. Corrosive chemicals include the sulfurous biproducts of gasoline engines and industrial contaminants. These materials can rapidly corrode metal components of furniture, especially brass, bronze, copper and silver, resulting in discoloration, pitting and, in severe cases, loss of the metal. Dust and dirt obscures the surface of furniture and hides decoration and color (Figure 9 A, B). Often, it has corrosive chemicals absorbed on its surface and these can attack and etch finishes and metals as described above. Additionally, dirt attracts and holds moisture against the surface, accelerating the types of deterioration associated with high relative humidity. Finally, dirt is abrasive and will scratch surfaces when they are rubbed during use or dusting.

Figure 9 A, B. The left side of both the painted blanket chest (9A) and the transparently-finished drawer front 9B) are covered with thick layers of dirt, obscuring the decoration and masking the colors. The right sides of both pieces have been cleaned.

It is easier to prevent the presence of dirt and pollutants than to rectify the damage caused by them. Institutions usually have HVAC (heating, ventilating, air conditioning) systems which have been designed to remove these contaminants. For smaller buildings and homes, system filters and room units are available. System filters attach directly to the air-handling unit of forced warm air heating systems, but can not be used with other types of heating plants. Individual room filtering units are available in an assortment of sizes, from table top to those capable of filtering large rooms or small houses. Each of the different models and brands has a differing effectiveness in removal of the specific contaminants in the air. For details, consult the specifications provided by the manufacturer of each unit under consideration, or confer with an air quality specialist. As a simple measure, covering pieces that are not on view with sheets of virgin polyethylene or unbleached muslin will help prevent dirt accumulation.

Biopredation

Biological attack of furniture occurs from two kingdoms, plant and animal. Plant predation is undertaken by a host of fungi, each of which can destroy a particular component of wood or associated materials. The least severe of these are the molds and mildews. They can attack and etch finishes and may stain the surface of wood in extreme cases, but otherwise are not likely to cause severe destruction (Figure 10). Other fungi, such as rots, for example, can reduce wood to a powder by consuming the lignin or cellulose in its structure. Such

Figure 10. Mold and mildew on a finish.

damage is permanent and irreversible. One of the most common of these is brown rot, commonly misnamed dryrot (Figure 11).

Spores of fungi are everywhere. They are extremely small and difficult to remove from the air by filtration. Therefore, given the appropriate growing conditions, fungi will thrive in virtually any building environment. Their primary need is a moisture source. This can be wood with a high moisture content, air of a high relative humidity, or moisture in floors or walls that are on or below ground level. Generally, fungi require warm temperatures between 50 and 100 degress Fahrenheit, although growth can occur outside both of these limits. Poor air circulation contributes to enhanced growth, primarily by allowing the existance of pockets of moist air.

The initial fungi control procedure is to remove the moisture source. Look for water leaks in the roof, walls and foundation, and eliminate them. Such sources of moisture guarantee that the relative humidity will be sufficiently high to allow fungal deterioration. Once they are removed, the relative humidity must be brought below about 70 percent to eliminate active growth. It should be recalled from the previous chapter that such a high level of RH is likely to cause other types of deterioration as well and maintenance of a constant level around 50 percent is advisable. If such conditions can be obtained, fungal growth will stop and the dried fruiting bodies can be carefully brushed off and vacuumed from the affected surfaces using appropriate

cleaniness procedures that prevent human irritation, such as gloves and a dust mask. The vacuum cleaner entraps the mold spores. If it is not possible to maintain the RH level properly, the objects should be removed from the room. Certain types of fumigants will kill fungi, but such a procedure will not prevent reinfestation and is unnecessary if environmental conditions are properly maintained. Cleaning disinfectants may harm the surfaces of wooden objects and should not be used unless they have been tested on the specific object in question by a conservator and found to be safe.

Insect infestation of wood, the major type of animal attack, is of two primary types; nesting and feeding. Nesting is done by carpenter ants, carpenter bees and a few other insects. These insects do not actually eat the wood for food, but chew it away to make cavities for hatching their young or for pupation. Their infestation of furniture and interior wooden objects is very rare. Normally, the cavities are near the surface and destruction of the wood is relatively minor (Figure 12).

Insects that feed on wood can totally destroy the structural integrity of a piece of furniture. Termites are found occasionally infesting wooden objects, usually if the object is in contact with a damp surface or the ground (Figure 13). Infestation by other types of wood-feeding insects is extremely common. Two well-known types are the powder post beetles, of which there are numerous species, and the furniture beetles. It is virtually impossible to distinguish between these different species unless an adult beetle or larvae is found, which is highly unlikely. Both of their life cycles are similar and begin with the female ovipositing eggs in a wood pore, crack or hole. The eggs hatch and the larvae eat channels roughly parallel to the grain direc-

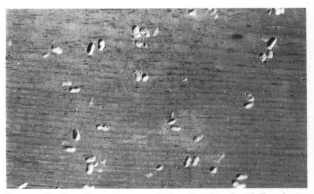

Figure 12. Pupal cavities made by the Arachnid Beetle in the inside of a drawer bottom that was lined with paper.

Figure 11. Rot on a barn sill that rests on the ground. The wood structure is so badly destroyed that a blunt screwdriver can be pushed completely through it.

Figure 13. Termite damage in the bottom of a box that rested on damp ground.

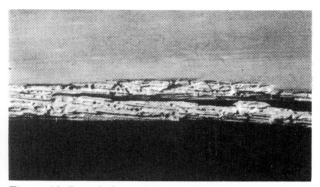

Figure 14. Larval channels primarily running parallel to the wood grain caused failure and separation of the board.

Figure 15 A, B. The surface of the board shows scattered flight holes (15 A). However, examination of the end reveals channels so extensive that the tenon crumbled away (15 B).

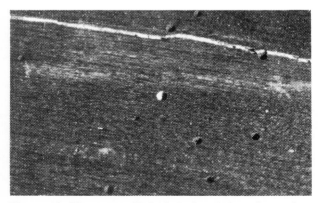

Figure 16. The center flight hole has light sides and is comparatively recent. The other holes have darkened sides.

tion inside the wood for a period which can be as long as several years, depending upon environmental conditions (Figure 14). When the larvae reach the pupal stage, they excavate a chamber near the surface of the wood. Upon emerging as adults, they chew a round exit or flight hole in the surface of the wood and fly or crawl away, often toward a light source such as a window. The adults mate and the cycle begins again with the female laying multiple eggs on a convenient piece of wood which is not necessarily the same piece from which she emerged. The surface appearance of the wood may belie the severity of the damage beneath it (Figure 15 A, B). Wood-boring beetle infestation of furniture is pervasive, especially in European furniture, where forgers have been known to add fake insect flight holes to simulate age.

The first step in control is detection of active infestation. Fresh flight holes will have edges that are the light color of unoxidized wood. Old hole sides will have darkened and are often filled with dust (Figure 16). One can fill existing flight holes with wax, allowing the definitive determination that a new hole without wax indicates activity. If infestation is suspected, inspect undisturbed places under and inside the object beneath flight holes for conical piles of frass, the dust-like byproducts of insect activity (Figure 17). Do not confuse abrasion from use and the dust it creates with frass. For further confirmation, a sheet of dark paper can be placed under the object and left undisturbed for up to several months. If piles of frass occur, current insect infestation is likely, although heavy vibrations in the building can cause frass to fall from old flight holes. Bear in mind throughout this whole investigation that there is no guarantee that active infestation is occurring near existing flight holes and the lack of dust does not mean necessarily the lack of insect activity.

If insect infestation is confirmed or only suspected, the pieces should be fumigated. In the meantime, placing them in totally sealed plastic bags or sheeting will temporarily suspend the spread of adults to other objects, although some insects can eat through the plastic. Currently, the fumigant of favor for historic objects is sulfuryl fluoride, manufactured by the Dow Chemical Company under the name Vikane. It must be applied by a licensed professional under controlled conditions, often a vacuum chamber, since all fumigants are as adept at killing humans as they are insects. In order to ensure egg kill, it is necessary to use a Vikane dosage that is 10 times the level recommended for drywood termites. As is true with any treatment, it is possible that the fumigant will react deleteriously with certain specific materials composing some objects. Be sure to consult the fumigant manufacturer's literature and with the licensed operator who will be doing the fumigation.

Figure 17. Piles of frass beneath flight holes.

Occasionally, rodents, canines and felines will prey on furniture (Figure 18). The former type of creature is usually exterminated, while the latter two are best treated with severe scolding or, respectively, with a bone or scratching post. Rodents are not eating the wood itself. Rather, they are chewing the wood to ingest something spilled on it or have a need to reach something on the other side of the board, such as a food supply or a nest.

This completes a brief investigation into the deterioration caused by light, environmental contaminants and biopredators. The succeeding chapter will focus on deterioration induced by furniture's largest and most difficult to control predator — man.

Figure 18. Rodent damage to the corner of a drawer.

Chapter 8

Furniture Deterioration: Man

The two previous chapters have examined the deterioration of furniture resulting from temperature, relative humidity fluctuations, light, contaminants, and biopredation. Many of these factors are indirectly a result of man's influence. The direct impact of man on deterioration of furniture — inherent vice, use and repairs — will be discussed in this chapter.

Inherent Vice

Inherent vice refers to deterioration that occurs due to design flaws by the maker of the piece of furniture, or because of limitations in the materials used. When considering design flaws by the maker, it is useful to recall from the preceding chapter on temperature and relative humidity that the environment in which 18th century cabinetmakers worked, for example, naturally was more stable for their pieces since central heating, along with its accompanying potential for vast swings in relative humidity, had not yet been invented. Naturally, they would not have perceived the problems faced by owners of furniture today. With this in mind, several manifestations of inherent vice will be examined.

The use of improperly seasoned wood can result in cracks and splits in a piece of furniture. If, for example, the environment is around 60 percent RH, wood would have an equilibrium moisture content of about 11 percent. If the wood used to build a piece is approximately this figure, the furniture will be in balance with its environment and no significant dimensional change will result, provided the environment remains constant. However, if the wood used is not fully seasoned, having, say an EMC of 20 percent, it will continue to shrink after

Figure 1
The top of this table was made from wood that was not fully seasoned. After being fashioned into a piece of furniture, continued shrinkage resulted in separation along the glue line.

the furniture is made, possibly resulting in splits (Figure 1).

Other inherent vice problems are related to unseasoned wood and wood movement as a result of environmental fluctuations, as illustrated by two examples. The drawers in some chests of drawers butt against the backboards when they are closed. This method of stopping the drawers is acceptable if the dimensions of the sides do not change. However, shrinkage of the sides results in drawers that do not fit in the now-shallower space (Figure 2). Such drawers that protrude from the

Figure 2
All of the drawers of this chest protrude about one quarter inch from the case due to side shrinkage.

front of a chest cannot be made flush once again without severe, and possibly unethical, structural alterations. Had the cabinetmaker used small wooden blocks for drawer stops instead of the backboards, the blocks could have been shaved to allow correct fitting of the drawers. A similar problem occurs when the drawer supports inside the case of a chest butt directly against the rails between the drawers. Shrinkage of the sides forces the rails out from the front of the chest (Figure 3). Provision of a small space of about 1/4 inch between the drawer support and the rail would have prevented this problem.

Unbalanced construction often results in distortion and warpage. If one side of a board is treated differently from the other, unbalanced construction is created. Common examples are veneer or finish on one surface and not on the opposite. When the ambient environment changes, the stresses on the two sides of the board are different and distortion can result. Unbal-

Figure 3
Side shrinkage without corresponding shrinkage of the drawer supports forced the rails out the front of the chest. This occurred because of negligable shrinkage of the longitudinal grain orientation of the drawer supports. Had the drawer supports been made with their long dimension in the tangential plane, an equivalent amount of support shrinkage may have prevented the illustrated damage. Another solution would have been to allow a space of around a quarter of an inch between the inside of the rail and the end of the drawer support.

anced construction is found frequently on crests of chests and mirrors (Figure 4). These surfaces were originally flat but curved backwards gradually in response to environmental fluctuations. Unbalanced construction is also created when one side of a board is exposed to circulating air and the other side is not, such as in the case of blanket chests and boxes. Environmental variations on the exposed side can create attempted dimensional change which is restrained by the opposite side of the board, resulting in compression setting, manifested as warpage (Figure 5).

Figure 5
The back of this box warped as a result of uneven air circulation on the inside and outside of the box.

Figure 4
This chest crest was originally flat and curved backwards as a result of fluctuating environmental conditions and unbalanced construction.

Finishes are subject to natural darkening and deterioration, although the amount varies greatly from one material to another and can be slowed in the proper environmental conditions. Darkening can reach a point where this inherent vice completely hides the wood surface (Figure 6). Viewing of the color and grain pattern

Figure 6
The color and grain pattern of the wood of this bookcase has been revealed only after the darkened finish has been removed on the top half.

is once again possible in most of these situations only by removal of the finish. Finishes can also lighten as they deteriorate (Figure 7).

Figure 7
The center of this panel finished with nitro-cellulose lacquer has lightened considerably. Fortunately, in this example, the damage was limited to the finish and the wood was unharmed.

Use

Furniture was made to be used. However, even careful use hastens deterioration. Severe use or misuse bring about extraordinarily rapid damage. It is important to remember that the greater the amount of use a piece of furniture receives, the greater will be the amount of deterioration.

Wear from use is one of the most common forms of deterioration. It can result in the loss of finishes, paints and of the wood itself. Common examples of problem areas are table tops, drawer runners, arms, seats and stretchers (Figure 8). Scratches can occur in finishes and in the wood surface (Figure 9). Stains, many of which can be removed only traumatically, occur commonly (Figure 10). Heat, often from pots or bodies, will

soften many finishes and may leave behind the impression of the heat source (Figure 11). Finally, when stresses from use or abuse exceed adhesive bond strength or wood strength, breakage occurs (Figure 12).

Of the types of chemical damage caused by use, water damage is by far the most common. Aqueous spills can etch finishes, resulting in a whitish opacity caused by the scattering of light instead of its transmission to the wood surface and reflection back to the

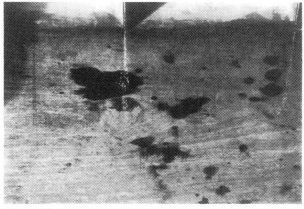

Figure 10
Ink stains on a desk. Many people consider such evidence of use as important historical documentation that should not be disturbed.

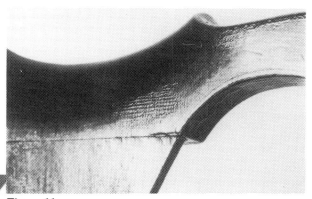

Figure 11
Impression of a fabric in the finish on the crest rail of a chair.

Figure 12
Stresses from use that were compounded at the hinge of this desk lid split the wood.

Figure 8
Loss of paint and surface wood from wear on the back stile of a Windsor chair.

Figure 9
Scratches in the finish of a chair stile.

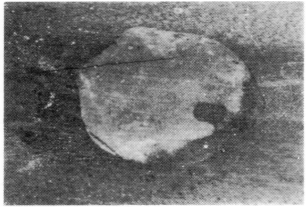

Figure 13
Water damage lightening a finish.

viewer's eye (Figure 13). Occasionally, the white area will disappear when the water dries, but normally the damage remains. Penetration of the water to the wood surface can create brownish-black marks in the wood cells on and below the surface (Figure 14). The depth of penetration depends on many factors but can reach a quarter inch or more. Extreme water contact with wood can remove the natural colorants from the wood (Figure 15) and swell the surface fibers, destroying the original contour and any patina that had been present (Figure 16). In addition to the deterioration mentioned above,

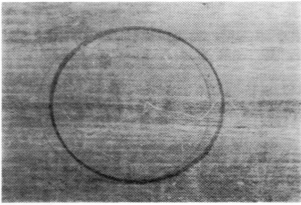

Figure 14
Water damage darkening the wood itself.

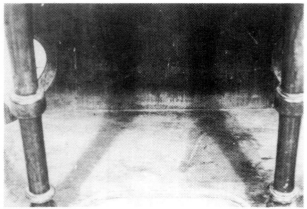

Figure 15
Natural wood colorants were leached by water immersion from the walnut base of this hall stand.

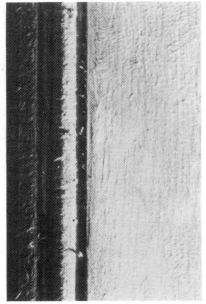

Figure 16
Water-induced swelling of wood fibers.

water in contact with wood will cause damage associated with increased moisture content, including compression setting and splitting, and will promote fungal attack. As a general rule, furniture and water should be kept as far apart as possible. Damage from water usually does not occur immediately upon contact. Often it is possible to wipe up quickly water spills without resulting negative effects.

Other chemicals will damage furniture, although the occurrance of such damage is less common than water-inflicted deterioration. Among the most common of household chemicals causing damage to furniture, acetone, found in nail polish remover, will dissolve certain finishes and alcohol is the solvent for shellac and other natural resins.

Repair

Improper repairs inflict damage that is particularly reprehensible, since such actions are completely unnecessary. Correction of improper repairs, if possible at all, is always much more time-consuming and expensive than if the repair had been done properly the first time. Damage from attempted repair is of two general types: improper materials and incorrect techniques. Examples of improper materials encompass the use of irreversible adhesives such as epoxies; finishes that darken and polymerize with age, such as linseed oil and polyurethane; and finish removers that damage the wood. Incorrect techniques include sanding during refinishing, the indiscriminate use of nails and screws, and sloppy workmanship. Attempt should **never be made to repair furniture** unless the repairperson has the proper materials, tools, and, most importantly, the proper knowledge.

Most structural repairs, including detachments, splits, breaks and separations, can be made with adhesives. The use of nails, screws, dowels or brackets is structurally unnecessary, ethically unacceptable, and — in most cases — produces additional damage by causing splitting and fragmenting of the wood (Figures 17A,B). Many adhesives, including hide glue that is

Figure 17A
Ten nails were driven into the endgrain of a structural member about the size of a 2 by 4, severely fragmenting it.

applied properly, are stronger than the wood itself. For this reason and because of their easy reversibility and long-term stability, hide glues, either traditional hot hide glue or modern liquid hide glue, are the choice for most reattachment needs (it is critical that liquid hide glues be applied and cured at temperature **above** 72 degress F). Additionally, hide glues are compatible with original hide glue residues. During a gluing process, it is important to ensure correct alignment of the

This misaligned pad foot is likely to suffer extensive damage if regluing is attempted. If a strong adhesive was used, the repair may not break at the glue line. Regardless, the extensive forces that would be necessary to attempt breakage are likely to damage the wood surface. Introducing a solvent deeply into a glue line can be difficult, if not impossible, even if the adhesive dissolves easily. In cases like this one, it may be best to learn to live with the poor repair.

Figure 18

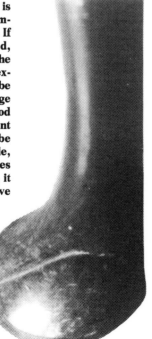

Figure 17B
The original dovetail joining of the rails of this recamier was destroyed by over-upholstery. The repairperson's solution was to fabricate and screw metal brackets to the leg, effectively changing the construction concept by transferring frame stresses to the leg, as well as producing unnecessary holes and potential weakening in the leg and framing members. When this repair failed, another repairperson fabricated a wooden crutch that was screwed to the framing members and went under the leg, lifting it about an inch higher than the other three legs. A better initial solution would have been to rebuild the fragmented dovetail joints, thereby once again reattaching the framing members to one another and producing a structurally sound object.

parts and to protect the object from marring due to clamping pressure with blocks beneath the clamps. Incorrectly aligned parts, even those adhered with reversible adhesives, can be virtually impossible to remove and realign without damaging the wood (Figure 18). To shave away the protruding portion of a misaligned repair must be condemned as unethical.

Improper refinishing is responsible for extensive damage to historic furniture. Incorrect finish removers can discolor wood surfaces and even degrade the wood. Ammonia, for example, will remove rapidly natural resin finishes; however, it is also a strong base and will darken severely many woods. Other solvents will bleach woods. Finish removal, when necessary, is best accomplished by using a solvent that is the mildest to both the object and the user. In a large percentage of cases, the appropriate solvent is denatured alcohol which effectively removes shellac and many other natural resins. Choice of the best solvent for finish removal is a process that requires a working knowledge of chemistry and should be referred to a conservator. Commercially prepared finish and paint removers include a whole host of solvents that dissolve virtually any coating that is encountered. Removers, in other words, contain solvents that are highly reactive and may be more dangerous than necessary not only to the furniture but also to the user. The use of any solvent must be accompanied by utilization of appropriate safety measures, including ventilation and the proper type of protective respirator and gloves.

The use of abrasives on the wood surface during refinishing is a common source of severe damage that is manifested as scratches, loss of patina, reduction in wood thickness and destruction of original surface contours (Figure 19). Wood that was smoothed by the cabinetmaker before application of the original finish still will be smooth hundreds of years later if it has not suffered from improper refinishing or unusually severe environmental conditions. It is not necessary normally, therefore, to sand after a degraded finish has been removed prior to the application of a new finish. It can be conjectured that employment of the destructive process of sanding during refinishing has evolved as a result of attention to books written for making new furniture, since freshly cut wood must be evened before satisfactory finishing results can be obtained. Home refinishers apparently interpreted the need to sand new work as a

Figure 20
The thick bottom boards of this piano had warped downwards. A repairperson drilled holes up into the carcase and inserted dowels, which were cut off very crudely with extensive saw damage to the wood. Ironically, the alignment after all of this work was completed was still unacceptable. The dowels were drilled out carefully, the surface between the bottom boards and the carcase cleaned of dirt and the two surfaces glued with hide glue. This simple repair, duplicating the original construction, produced much better alignment, was stronger, did not create severe damage to the object and required less time.

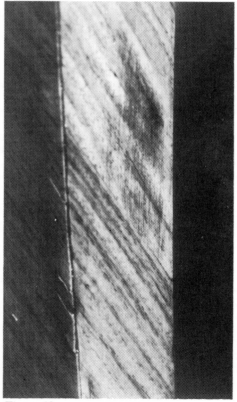

Figure 19
Sanding scratches in veneer. The previously-existing oxidised, patinated surface can be seen under the scratches as contrasted with the "skinned" appearance of new wood surrounding it.

need to sand during refinishing, thereby damaging untold numbers of wooden objects.

Application of inappropriate finishes accounts for further damage to furniture. Linseed oil and other drying oils, while being easy to apply, also penetrate into the surface wood cells. As they age, they polymerize into a single huge molecule, becoming less soluble and darker, and reaching a stage in a relatively few years where their removal threatens damage to the surface of the wooden object itself. Polyurethane varnishes similarly crosslink and become less soluble upon aging. Shellac, on the other hand, is the finish used most often by conservators, because it remains easily soluble as it ages and can be applied by rag (French polishing), brush or spray. Furthermore, a refining process that removes the naturally-occuring waxes results in a shellac, called blonde dewaxed, that is harder and more resistant to water damage.

The final type of damage from improper repair that will be addressed in this article is poor workmanship. Common examples include the removal and discarding of huge portions of furniture because repairpersons can make only ill-fitting replacement parts; inflicted saw or chisel damage next to repairs; lack of adequate knowledge to fix furniture properly; or blatant violation of the integrity of furniture such as by the cutting off of feet to reduce the height of a chair or the trimming of moldings to allow a cupboard to fit a smaller space (Figure 20). Both the repairpersons and the furniture owners involved in integrity assassination should, in all fairness, be subjected to the same fate as the furniture!

This chapter concludes an examination of the nature of furniture and the forces that promote its deterioration. The final chapter will summarize preservation issues and present additional suggestions for the care and maintenance of furniture and wooden objects.

Chapter 9

Summary of Furniture Preservation and Care

The profession of furniture conservation had its roots in the woodworking tradition. Early repair was done by carpenters, who were the makers of the pieces as well. By the 18th century, cabinetmaking had developed as an occupation distinct from carpentry and joinery. Examinations of surviving cabinetmaker's account books of this period show repair of furniture to be one of the services they offered. At this time, though, it is doubtful that the economic and social structures had allowed the development of full-time repairpersons. The late 19th century was characterized by an intense discovery of the past, with its subsequently engendered desire for "things old." A flourishing group of repairers, restorers and forgers was afforded an existance by this change in societal attitude.

By the 1930s, scientific examination was being applied to works of fine art and the materials used for their restoration in order to understand better deterioration and preservation issues. This was the beginning of the true profession of conservation. By the 1960s, the transformation from restoration to ethical conservation had begun to occur in the furniture field. Today, even though great strides forward have been made, there is still an abundance of misinformation about furniture deterioration, restoration and care being presented to the public in books and by personal contact with cabinetmakers, repairpersons and restorers who have not adjusted yet to the shift to conservation philosophy.

One attempt to create basic standards of conservation professionalism is the American Institute for Conservation's *Code of Ethics and Standards of Practice*. The Code is embraced by most conservators as a guide for their approach to the treatment and care of historic objects, including furniture. The major concepts of the Code as applied to furniture follow.

Respect for the inherent integrity of the object must be held supreme by the conservator. The conservator does not have the right to alter or destroy the original or historic fabric of the object or evidence of original manufacturing techniques. The conservator should intervene minimally on the remaining original surfaces, and his/her work should not be confused with the original.

The conservator strives to use treatment materials that are reversible and can be removed in the immediate or distant future. All materials deteriorate and even in the best of circumstances, retreatment of the object will be necessary eventually. Conservators are concerned with the safety of the materials used to the furniture and also do not want the eventual degradation products of these materials to damage the piece. Therefore, only well-tested, highly stable materials are used ordinarily. Since it is important to differentiate the work of the conservator from the original, the conservator may choose to use materials that are dissimilar to those used by the maker.

Each piece of furniture is unique, and so is its state of deterioration. Even two pieces made by the same person at the same time will have differences in the original construction and appearance as well as have suffered varying types of degradation with the passing of time. For any given specific deterioration problem, there may be several possible (and equally ethically acceptable) treatment options. For these reasons, the conservator must weigh the needs of each specific piece of furniture prior to recommending a treatment. It follows that personal examination of the object by the conservator is a necessity.

Prior to beginning treatment of a piece of furniture, the conservator must document its condition. This is done with a written condition report that is usually accompanied by photographs. Following treatment, the conservator produces a treatment report that lists the specific materials and processes used.

The variety and complexity of materials used for the construction of furniture requires that the conservator be aware of recent developments in the conservation profession. Additionally, the conservator has an obligation to be involved with increasing the pool of conservation understanding by researching and writing and to pass his/her knowledge on to others by teaching.

Wood, of which the majority of furniture is composed, is an extremely complex material. Specialists have spent their entire careers studying one small aspect of wood and still do not understand it completely. While it is impossible, therefore, to predict exactly what will happen to a specific piece of furniture with the passage of time, a general understanding of the nature of wood allows determination of characteristic causes of deterioration. Wood is anisotropic — its properties are not uniform and are dependent upon the orientation of its cells. The most important of wood's many anisotropic properties to deterioration of furniture is its dimensional response to variations in moisture content. During the seasoning process, as wood's moisture content drops below the fiber saturation point, bound water is given up until the remaining bound water in the wood is in equilibrium with the relative humidity of the surrounding air. Corresponding with the loss of the bound water is shrinkage of the wood. The amount is affected by the way the wood was cut from the tree. Shrinkage in wood from the tangential plane can exceed 10 percent, while radial plane shrinkage is roughly half this amount. Longitudinal shrinkage normally does not exceed 1/10 percent. As the relative humidity of the environment rises, wood absorbs moisture and expands. Conversely, when the RH falls, wood gives up moisture and contracts. This process occurs regardless of the age of the wood.

The response of dimensional variation with cycling relative humidity directly manifests itself as damage to furniture. Boards allowed to move unrestrained will suffer, at worst, checking at the ends of the boards and warpage. However, when the construction of a piece of furniture inhibits free movement, such as cross-grain attachment of wooden members to one another, more severe degradation can result. If attempted shrinkage is prohibited, boards (and veneer) can split. Restricted expansion can result in compression setting of the wood — the physical squeezing together of the wood cells. Returning the board to its original moisture content results in a board that is permanently smaller and possibly split due to restrained shrinkage. The stresses generated by dimensional changes in wood are easily great enough to fracture glue joints with resulting joint looseness and loss of parts. Prevention of damage to historic wooden objects from dimensional variation of wood can be accomplished only by stabilizing the temperature and relative humidity of the object's ambient environment.

Environmental factors other than temperature and relative humidity have deleterious effects on wood. Light will bleach the natural colorants found in wood, as well as the original coloring agents applied by the cabinetmaker. In addition, ultraviolet light can damage the cells on and near the surface of wood. Light will cause rapid degradation of finishes, bleaching and severely crazing them and, in severe cases, will result in their cleavage from the wood and loss. Damage from light is not reversible, so furniture should be kept in the lowest light level possible. It is especially important to eliminate ultraviolet light, large proportions of which are contained in sunlight and most fluorescent light bulbs.

Dirt not only obscures the appearance and colors of the surface of furniture, but also contains chemicals that can attack finishes and metal components. Insect infestation, commonly by the larvae of powder post beetles and of furniture beetles, can weaken wood so severely that it is unable to support its own weight. Early detection and fumigation are the solution to such infestations. It is important to bear in mind that adult beetles fly and females can lay eggs on pieces of furniture or other wooden surfaces far from the infested one, so quick action once the problem is discovered is imperative.

Furniture's largest and most damaging pest — man — is also the hardest to control, as fumigation generally is not considered acceptable treatment. Education, while much slower, is a more humane solution to this problem. The issue of damage to furniture caused by man is complicated by the fact that furniture is intended to be used, yet even the most careful use hastens deterioration. Minimization of damage can be accomplished by understanding the limitations and weaknesses of each piece of furniture and using it well within these limitations. In general, this consists of careful use, proper environmental conditions, correct maintenance procedures, and, when necessary, ethical and properly conducted repair and treatment.

Care and Maintenance

Ideal environmental conditions for the preservation of furniture are constant relative humidity of 50 percent, constant temperature of about 45 degrees F, total darkness, no dirt or pollutants in the air, lack of insect infestation, and no handling or use. In most situations, these conditions are impractical. Therefore, it is important to vary from these levels as little as possible, with the knowledge that the amount of deterioration an object will suffer will be directly proportional to the deviation from ideal environmental levels. If one approaches these ideals, the need for additional care or maintenance virtually is eliminated. Rephrased. care and maintenance of furniture consists, first and foremost, of providing the proper environment. Additional procedures only compensate for failings in the previous or current environments.

Cleaning

Loose dust on a piece of furniture can be removed with a clean, soft, dry cloth gently rubbed over the surface. Dust is an abrasive and excess pressure can scratch the finish. Do not attempt cloth dusting of a surface that is severely deteriorated. Cloth fibers may catch and tear away pieces of the finish, veneer or loose parts (Figure 1). Such areas may be able to be dusted with a clean natural bristle paint or artist's brush. Watch carefully for loss of surface and stop if it is observed, refer-

Figure 1 - Loose brass inlay was caught by a feather duster, pulled out of its groove and bent. Often, such pieces break away and are lost. Similar problems occur with cloths when dusting objects with surfaces that show signs of deterioration.

ring the problem to a conservator. Surfaces **in good condition** with heavy accumulations of dust can be cleaned carefully with a vacuum cleaner. Use the lowest suction that is effective and the dusting brush attachment. Do not let metal or hard plastic parts of the vacuum contact the surfaces, or scratches in the finish and wood may result. Damage to furniture occurs commonly as its feet and bases are struck while the floor is being vacuumed. These seemingly insignificant impacts have a severe cumulative effect, resulting in loss of wood and finishes.

More securely attached dirt on finished surfaces **in good condition** may be removed with surfactants which are mixed in a dilute solution with distilled or deionized water. Common types are Orvus Liquid (available from many tack shops), Igepal, Triton X-100 and Vulpex. If a local source can not be found, surfactants can be ordered from Conservation Materials, Box 2884, 340 Freeport Blvd., Sparks, NV 89431. A small spot in an obscure area is tested with the solution on a cotton swab. All areas that appear to be a different surface coating or material must be tested separately. If the solution does not damage the test area, it can be used to clean the piece. A soft cloth is dampened **slightly** and rubbed over the surface. Avoid excessive wetting of the surface, which may cause the types of damage associated with water. The cleaned surface should be wiped with a soft cloth dampened slightly with plain distilled or deionized water to remove surfactant residues, followed by a dry soft cloth. Finished surfaces that show deterioration or bare wood should not be cleaned with water solutions of surfactants and should be referred to a conservator.

Dirt on surfaces **in good condition** that does not respond to surfactant cleaning may be removable with organic solvents. When using solvents, it is a good practice to have plenty of ventilation and to wear gloves and a respirator approved for use with the specific solvent. Also beware of solvent flammability. The first solvent to try to mineral spirits, commonly sold as paint thinner. If mineral spirits is unsuccessful, VM&P naptha would be the next solvent to test. These two solvents will remove waxes, so do not use them on pieces with wax finishes unless their removal is the desired result. Other solvents may be successful cleaning agents, but they are also stronger and able to remove certain finishes. Therefore, if mineral spirits and VM&P naptha are unsuccessful, the cleaning problem should be referred to a conservator. Solvent cleaning proceeds much the same way as surfactant cleaning — an inconspicuous area should be tested with solvent on a swab for effectiveness and safety to the piece. Test all areas that appear to be different. If cleaning can proceed, lightly moisten a wad of cotton, lint-free pad, such as a lithographer's pad, or soft cloth with the appropriate solvent. Follow with a clean, dry cloth. Since all the solvent will evaporate, it is unnecessary to rinse the cleaned area. Remember, if the surface is deteriorated, cleaning should be referred to a conservator.

Polishing

Finished surfaces do not require any treatment to help preserve them other than provision of good environmental conditions. Polishes do not prevent finish deterioration. At best, they visually compensate for degradation that has occurred already and, at worst, they rapidly accelerate finish deterioration. The two common types of polishes are oils and waxes. Oils are of two general groups — drying oils such as linseed oil and tung oil, and non-drying oils like mineral oil, paraffin oil and lubricating oils. Drying oils react with oxygen in the air and polymerize, forming, in effect, one giant molecule which requires very harsh solvents to remove. Combined with the polymerization is a darkening of the oil and the entrapment of dust and dirt, resulting in an oil layer that is so blackened that the underlying wood is completely obscured. The subsequent removal of the oil may damage or destroy the finish beneath it (Figure 2). Unfortunately, a number of museums in the 1960s and 1970s were recommending the use of furniture polishes containing linseed oil, vinegar and turpentine. It is now realized that these polishes are quite harmful, but the recipes are still

Figure 2 - The wood color and grain of the leg of this table has been obscured over much of its surface by darkened residues of linseed oil polish. The grain can be seen showing through the polish in the light areas of the leg.

recommended in published sources. Drying oils, such as linseed and tung oils, **should not be used** on historic furniture.

Non-drying oils are often found in commercially-prepared furniture polishes, such as the misnamed "lemon" oil, which is usually paraffin oil with added perfumes. These oils and polishes containing them are easy to apply and look good after the first few applications, although the surface treated with them will feel oily since they do not dry chemically. After repeated applications, such oils can become gummy and entrap dirt, resulting in a surface that is sticky and streaky. In order to try to even this appearance, non-drying oils must be applied more and more frequently. Finally, chemical removal of the residues is necessary, with a great potential for damage to the underlying finish (Figure 3, A, B). It is recommended that all oils, both drying and non-drying, be kept far from historic furniture and wooden objects.

Waxes are among the most stable materials known. Beeswax found in the tombs of Egypt was in such good condition that it was indistinguishable chemically from its modern counterpart. Waxes remain on the surface of objects and can be removed easily with mild solvents. Therefore, if it is desirable to enhance the appearance of a mildly degraded finish, waxes are the materials of choice. Additionally, waxes can give added resistance

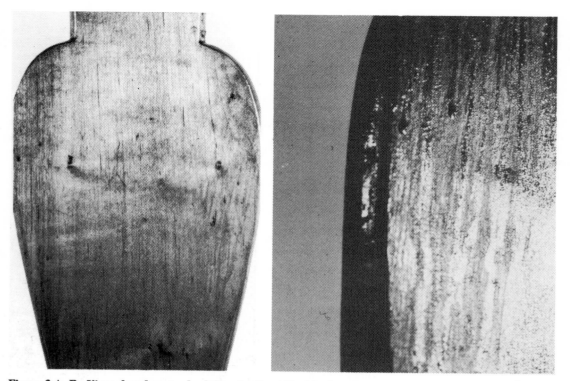

Figure 3 A, B - Viewed under standard illumination (A), this chair back appears normal. However, when viewed in reflected light (B), gummy accumulations and streaks caused by oil polish can be seen clearly.

to water damage to finishes that are susceptible to it. Any of the commercially-available paste waxes (not liquid) are acceptable, provided they contain only waxes and a solvent, such as mineral spirits or turpentine. Commonly available brands are Renaissance, Johnson's, Butcher's, Minwax and Mowhawk. Avoid any product that contains silicones, as they are nearly impossible to remove from the surface once applied and will interfere with future treatment attempts by prohibiting the bonding of coatings and finishes (Figure 4). Apply the paste wax following the manufacturer's directions on the can. After drying, the wax is buffed

Figure 4 A, B - The protective coating applied over the decoration of this papier-mache chair back was not able to adhere properly because of silicone contamination of the surface from polishes (A). Note the islands of coating, indicating surface tension repulsion. Ultimately, the coating will peal from the surface (B).

with a soft cloth to an even sheen. Too frequent wax application will result in thick deposits in recesses and corners. In most situations, it is not necessary to re-apply wax more often than every one to three years. Occasional buffing between applications will even streaks that may appear from use.

Nicks and Scratches

It is best to consult with a conservator before attempting treatment of furniture nicks and scratches. In lieu of a conservator's advice, pigmented wax is a safe method of reversibly hiding such damage. Artist's dry pigments can be blended with a moderately soft wax to achieve a good color match. This usually necessitates melting the wax in a double boiler — beware of flammability. Pigments also can be blended into paste wax without heating, although the fill will shrink as the solvents in the paste wax evaporate and repeated applications will be necessary. Pre-colored wax pencils are available at hardware stores. While being more convenient, they are available in a limited range of colors. Solid waxes will have to be melted into the damaged area with a low temperature melt-in knife, available from finishing suppliers or by heating a metal spatula or similar implement.

An alternative for damage that does not require filling but only color matching are artist's acrylic paints that are designed specifically to be reversible. Different colors can be mixed to produce the best color match with the damaged area. Acrylics are applied with artist's brushes and dry to a matte appearance. Dilution to a thinner working consistency, and removal at a future time can be done with toluene and other organic solvents (use a respirator). Gloss can be increased by topcoating with Acryloid B-72, made by Rohm and Haas (Acryloids and reversible acrylic paints are available from Conservation Materials and other suppliers). Another coloring option is to mix dry artist's pigments directly in Acryloid B-72 and apply them in the same manner as acrylic paints.

Hardware

Currently, in the art historical community, there is a raging debate on the advisability of polishing metal furniture hardware. If one chooses to polish, remove the hardware from the piece, being sure to note the exact location of each screw and nut. Polishing hardware on the piece abrades the surrounding finish and allows polishing agents to run beneath the hardware where they can damage the metal and the finish. Additionally, polish residues left on the surface of hardware can cause corrision (Figure 5). After polishing, coat the hardware with Acryloid B-72, or for severe useage, with Incralac or Acryloid B-48N (available from Conservation Materials and other suppliers). These coatings will prolong greatly the time between polishings. Do not polish gilt or plated hardware.

Myths

It is important to understand that a number of myths about wood and the care of furniture still are being propagated. Since they are contained in published articles and books, dispelling these myths is extremely difficult. Hopefully, this booklet has provided the reader with an understanding of furniture and wood that corrects such misconceptions. At the risk of being redundant, the myths now will be exposed and purged from the face of the earth!

Figure 5 - Note the light shadows on the finish surrounding this applied mount. These are regions of finish damage from metal polishes.

Myth #1: "Wood is alive." Wood is **not** alive. Even in the living tree, the vast majority of wood cells are dead. When the tree is cut, the few remaining living cells die. By the time furniture is made from lumber cut from trees, the wood has been dead for a long time.

Myth #2: "Wood needs to breathe and applying coatings such as waxes suffocates it." Wood **does not** breathe. There is no need to have free air circulation at the surface of wood and coating wood with finishes will not cause damage to the wood.

Myth #3: "Wood and finishes need to be fed." Wood and finishes **do not** need to be fed or nourished. Wood is not alive and, therefore, can not need food. Wood that is unfinished or existing finishes that are dirty and somewhat deteriorated appear dry and "lifeless." The optical saturation and depth of colors characteristic of a freshly-applied finish are not present. This is purely a visual phenomonon and does not indicate that the wood is deteriorated or in need of sustinance. If aesthetic enhancement is desired (it is not required for preservation), unfinished wood can have a reversible finish applied and existing finishes can be cleaned and waxed.

Myth #4: "As wood ages, it loses moisture and natural wood oils, which need to be periodically replaced (usually with the favorite oil polish or feeder of the expounder)." Most woods **do not** have oils. Of the few that do, the oils in no way affect the preservation of the wood and adding oil (which, as a matter of fact, is not the same oil as that present in the wood) will not have positive effects on preservation, as described above. The amount of moisture in wood is directly controlled by the relative humidity and temperature of the surrounding air. Wood **can not lose** moisture if it is at equilibrium moisture content with the ambient environment unless the relative humidity falls or the temperature rises. Adding moisture to wood in an attempt to replace that which has been "lost" will cause a temporary rise in moisture content which will immediately begin to fall until it again reaches equilibrium with the environment. This rapid moisture content rise and fall may cause damage to the wood in the form of compression setting and splitting. Certain proponents of oil polishes claim that the oil itself replaces moisture lost from wood. This is blatantly incorrect. Oil can not enter the cellular structure to substitute for water; in fact, oil is hydrophobic (water-fearing) and is repelled by water.

Conclusion

Prevention of damage to furniture and wooden objects is best facilitated by provision of good environmental conditions, including careful use. Periodic application of polishes or "preservatives" is not necessary. At best, these materials compensate for damage that has occurred already or, in the case of waxes, can provide additional protection from water damage. At worst, they can accelerate greatly deterioration of surfaces and possibly require damage to the wood for their eventual removal.

Choosing A Conservator

Even with the best of care, furniture occasionally may need the attention of a furniture conservator. Choosing such an individual can be a difficult undertaking. There are three areas to consider in making such a decision: the individual's training, his/her ethical orientation and professional involvement, and, finally, his/her hand skills.

Three primary training options for furniture conservators are apprenticeship, graduate conservation program or equivalent, and self-directed study. The quality of apprenticeship training depends primarily upon the knowledge and skills of the supervisor. Generally, only one perspective is given, but a dedicated apprentice can supplement this with extensive readings and attendance at conferences, courses and workshops. Analytical skills and ethical orientation can be lacking in apprenticeship training. Graduate programs provide a wide, well-rounded exposure to conservation with the perspectives of a number of conservators and scientists presented to the student. Ethical orientation is stressed, as are problem solving and analysis. Self-directed study places the entire burden of training on the individual. If the student is highly motivated, he/she can combine college courses with internships, self-study, and attendance at workshops and conferences to provide a good conservation background. However, it is often difficult for these individuals to gain access to highly-qualified conservators to teach them.

A conservator's ethical orientation can be determined by educating oneself in the basics of conservation. Obtain and read the American Institute for Conservation's *Code of Ethics and Standards of Practice* (AIC, 3545 Williamsburg Lane, NW, Washington, DC 20008, 202-364-1036) and *Furniture Care and Conservation* by Robert McGiffin. Professional journals, such as

the *AIC Journal* and *Studies in Conservation* (International Institute for Conservation [IIC], 6 Buckingham St., London WC2N 6BA, England) will give a more indepth approach to typical conservation problems.

Attendance at conservation seminars and conferences provides not only contact with conservators, but also a more thorough understanding of the whole profession. Towards this end, join AIC as an associate member and attend their annual conference. Other organizations that could be helpful to join are the American Association of Museums (AAM), IIC, the American Association for State and Local History (AASLH), the National Institute for Conservation of Cultural Property (NIC), and the International Council of Museums: Committee for Conservation (ICOM).

With a good conservation understanding, one should ask many questions of a prospective conservator. Inquire about their ethical orientation and professional memberships. Present them with hypothetical situations to which one knows the answer and carefully evaluate their response (remember, most situations have more than one acceptable solution). Inquire about their training and experience. Be sure to discuss the specifics of the condition and treatment of one's piece of furniture. During the entire conversation, listen for substance, not salesmanship.

Evaluation of a conservator's hand skills can be quite difficult before they work on one's piece. Begin by asking the opinions of conservators at major local museums. Curators also can be approached, but be cautioned that many curators may be swayed overly by the appearance of a piece of furniture after conservation work, rather than by the ethical constraints of the profession. Enlightened former clients may be able to offer opinions. Finally, visit the conservation facility and observe treatments that are in progress. Look for respect being shown to the furniture. Tools should not be placed on the pieces, nor should the conservators rest their body parts upon the furniture.

Once a conservator has been chosen, one should expect a courteous, professional attitude. The conservator should listen to one's needs and provide several options to solve the furniture's problems. Be wary of anyone who is pushy about a single solution without having solid facts to back it up. One should receive straightforward information from the conservator and no talk of magic or secret formulas. If one hears about living, breathing, hungry wood — run! The conservator should adhere to the AIC *Code of Ethics* or a similar ethical code.

A condition report and proposed treatment report should be received before any conservation treatment is begun. These documents outline the nature and location of deterioration and the specific materials and techniques that will be used to remedy the problems. Included should be an estimate of cost. Following treatment, a treatment report should be submitted, listing in detail the materials and processes used on the piece during treatment. Photographs of the piece before and after treatment should be provided, including close-ups of specific areas of deterioration. A brochure available from AIC entitled "Guidelines for Selecting a Conservator" provides additional helpful information.

There are no easy solutions to choosing a conservator. It requires basic knowledge and education in conservation issues. The problem of poor treatment of historic objects has been with society for centuries. In the words of Thomas Hoving in the June 1987, issue of *Connoisseur*, "... there's nothing like continuing publicity to keep conservators on their toes and accountable. In the past, 'restorers' have quietly wrecked more monuments than Genghis Kahn did.'' Understanding of proper conservation and maintenance needs can help prevent this needless loss of our cultural heritage.

One of the fuctions of the Conservation Analytical Laboratory of the Smithsonian Institution is to assist in the dissemination of conservation information to the public. The Information Department can be reached at 202-287-3712. Please have your question clearly formed before calling. Be aware that questions about the treatment of specific objects are difficult, if not impossible, to answer without personal examination by a conservator.